THE IRRESISTIBLE BUSINESS PLAN & GRANT WRITING MADE EASY

BY: MICHAEL J. CLINTON

DRAXUM PUBLISHING

LEARNING

DRAXUM PUBLISHING
2 Haven Plaza * New York 10009

Copyright © 2014 by Draxum Publishing
Book Cover Design by: Eugene Rodriguez

Table of Contents

Target Market
Resources
How to Write a Company Description
Factors to Consider When Writing a Company Description

Market Research- What is it?
Different Types Of Market Research
Categories Involved In A Market Research

Four Key Benefits of Organizational Structure
The right time to work on your Organizational Structure
Key Elements Of Organizational Structure
The Basic Business Structure
Conclusion

The Design
Product Position
The Approach
The Market
The Margin
Your Competition

Build Your Internet Marketing Plan
General Rules of Marketing Your Product
How Successful Marketers do it Differently

Your Savings
Family and Friends
Grants

INTRODUCTION

The Irresistible Business Plan and Grant Writing Made Easy is a simple one-two punch for individuals who are interested in writing a business plan for their for-profit enterprise or seeking funding for their non-profit organization.

Oftentimes, people who are interested in starting a business or a non-profit don't know the first thing about a business plan or grant writing, which automatically puts you at a disadvantage. If you don't know how to write a business plan or request funding via a grant, you'll either have to pay someone to write it for you, drudge your way thru a course or buy a book with 350 plus pages on one of the subjects and here's the kicker, you probably won't even read the entire book. If you have the time for that, that's great, if you don't, consider this book your "cliffs notes".

This easy to read book will allow you to put together an affective business plan and afterwards a grant request without the agony and stress of conquering a gigantic imaginary scholarly undertaking. We're not talking about splitting an atom or defining the center of gravity, in other words, it isn't rocket science. You can do this yourself if you so desire.

Every business wants to save money and cut cost. By writing your own business plan or grant request, you actually get to do that and more importantly, you get to know your business... or learn how it's done and help someone else know his or hers.

CHAPTER 1

WHY YOU NEED A BUSINESS PLAN

The reason every business, small or big, needs a business plan? What is the underlying potential of having a realistic, objective and unemotional business guide?

A business plan is just like a blue print for your business. When you are planning to build a house, you wouldn't just walk into an empty lot and start putting bricks and wood together, you would need to have a plan on how to build it. In the same way, a business is a huge project that needs a guide to follow.

Unlike a house once it's completed, a business is not static. It is prone to changes in the future. A business plan is one of the most crucial steps to start a business. Get it right, and you will reap unbelievable trust from investors, staff, distributers and agencies. Get it wrong, and your business can sink faster than a *wiseguy'* with two cement blocks tied to his feet.

So What Is A Business Plan?

- A business plan is a detailed document that explains exactly how and why you are running the business. It will include how you will be promoting your business, how you plan on funding your business, how you will find investors and who your customers will be.

- Your business plan is also your financial prediction in which you will be calculating the amount needed to start the venture, how much profit you think will come in. It will also state how you are planning to make your profit, how you will raise your funds and how many rounds of financial funding you might need.
- Considering the market for your business, your business plan will include a detailed market research on how your competitors are doing, and your target audience. You will categorize your market research depending on the information that you gather from your target audience's spending habits, earning capability, core interest areas, age and their socializing groups.
- Most business plans have a section which explains in detail the number of employees needed for the business to start out, how many you are going to hire in the future and the salary you will be able to pay them. This financial forecast will help your investors understand the financial commitment they may be getting into.
- You should write your business plan in such a way that it is capable of being updated regularly taking into account whatever the economic scenario might be, the industry scale and the direction your business is intending to follow.

How Important Is A Business Plan?

Writing a business plan does not mean that you hide away in some dark corner of a library to put together a 40 plus page book. You can make up a business plan in less than a month, provided that you are completely clear on your business idea. Since everything is turning digital, you can use a PowerPoint presentation or Keynote to save all your thoughts and store them. Saving them digitally makes it easier to erase and make edits.

Here Are Some Benefits Of Putting Together A Business Plan:

Avoid Mistakes

There's one thing you don't want to hear when you start your own business or company and that is, "You made a mistake." What that typically means is that you have to amend, modify or make changes to your entire business strategy just to get it back to ground zero. Many first time business owners have learned the hard way either because they couldn't set aside enough capital to reach their goals or they hooked up with ineffectual partners who did not have adequate skills and resources, or they didn't have a concrete way to earn money. Writing down a business plan will give you an idea on how to plan your future based on your financial resources, the skills that are require and the money you need to generate.

Emotional Equilibrium

If you are a first time business owner, chances are that you will panic even at the smallest issues. Perhaps, you are so passionate about your idea that you lose sight of reality and work impractically. Other times you will be frustrated, tensed, stressed, doubtful, or maybe even fearful. When your emotions take hold of you, it's your business plan that can keep you from wigging out and give you strength. It lets you take a realistic look at your objective, the reason for your condition, the actual facts of the situation and the solution to the problem.

Direction

Chances are that you are not starting your business alone. You might have a partner, a board of directors, a superior authoritative power or your friends, family and advisers. A business plan is the best way to explain everything about the business to everyone and make everyone head in the same direction. If you do not have a business plan, you might have to explain, remind, suggest and advise people about your business strategy again and again, which can be a pain in the neck. A business plan will alleviate all of that.

Game plan

Execution is the key to all start-ups. This means you have to set priorities, measure performance levels and define goals. Answering key questions like; what does my customer really want? How much will they spend on my product? Will they even be remotely interested in buying my product? The answers to these questions will give you a clear idea on how you will be executing your business. You might also have to identify the ways in which you will attract your customers and convince them to buy your product.

Capital

Beg, borrow or steal – whatever you do, it needs a plan. You will have to clearly communicate your business in a detailed and compelling way. A good business plan will help you do just that. To start a business you will need operating as well as startup capital and no financial institution is going to give you money without a proper business plan. In fact, if you have a rich friend, he or she will want to see a business plan. Why? Unless they hit the lottery, they didn't become rich on some whimsical business venture. They are more than likely savvy professionals.

Even an established business that needs further funding has to develop a business plan in order to get financial assistance. Having a business plan will give you a better opportunity to win the heart of investors and/or financial institutions.

Practicality

Most often people are so passionate about their new business that they become over optimistic. Writing down a business plan is the best way to judge if your ideas are practical and easy to carry out. Your business plan is your safety net which can save you a lot of time, effort and money as it reveals if your idea is practical or not. Often a business strategy is abandoned at the marketing stage or the competitive analysis stage only to free you to move on to perhaps bigger better ideas.

Better Success

A business plan is all about seeing the bigger picture at one go and analyzing its potential to success. A business plan when written down can be assessed more critically and steps can be taken to bring in more profit. Mostly when people go ahead with their instincts and skip the business plan, there's a huge chance that they might not find the solution to all the unseen emergencies. This is where a person with a business plan can succeed and move ahead to find better success.

Effective Operations

Businesses are dynamic and are subjected to changes and growth. Being ready for such phases of the business is important for effective operations. Moreover, as the business grows, more employees will undoubtedly need to be hired, the management has to be arranged and effective operational plans need to be made. A business plan can sort this out.

Office Space

If you are acquiring office space, that's a huge investment you're talking here. If you can convert your home to your office space, you can save a lot on your expenses and rent. This expenditure cannot be overlooked under any circumstances. Sometimes we overlook such things and get into trouble with our finances. A business plan will cover all such things and will help you to sort out your expenses.

Your Personal Business Plan Checklist:

- ✓ Business detail on how and why your business will run.
- ✓ All financial records, predictions and investment plans.
- ✓ A complete detailed market research.
- ✓ Updates in business plan when required.
- ✓ How many employees you will need during the start up and an expected number in future.
- ✓ The practicality of the idea.
- ✓ The future of the business and its potential growth.
- ✓ Business development perspective of the entire venture.
- ✓ Management of cash flow.

HERE ARE ANSWERS TO A FEW TYPICAL QUESTIONS YOU MIGHT HAVE

I don't need an investor. Do I still need a business plan?

Of course you do! Contrary to the common beliefs, a business plan is made not just to secure your investment, but is a map for you to follow precisely to reach your goal. A business plan is a step-by-step instruction to follow in a particular direction without getting diverted.

I know my business all too well. Do I still need a plan?

Sometime, when we get too passionate about our business, chances are that we tend to get carried away and forget practicality. There are few entrepreneurs who don't dream of having a million dollar business. Letting our emotions take hold of our conscious gets us deviated from the main focus and then we end up in trouble. If we have a business plan we can take a step back and follow it with sober eyes, as it is, a realistic unemotional guide to success.

My business is too small. Do I still need a business plan?

Yes you do. Every business small or big needs a business plan because the core concept of a business is profit and success. To achieve this, one needs to have a concrete plan on how to reach their goal and attain success.

Are all 'business plans' the same?

Each business is unique and no two business plans can be identical. The way you perceive a business and wish to carry it forward will be totally different from a person who wishes to do the same business. Although, you might be selling the same product as that of your competitor, you still need a strategy on how to outdo them and grow your business bigger.

Should I consult my business plan with anybody?

Sharing your business plan with someone you trust is a good idea, as it will give you rational input on what is wrong and what is right. As long as you are sure that the person is trustworthy and knows something about business, you can ask them for their honest opinion and work on areas that they think might be impractical. But always be aware of your friends that may have a pessimistic outlook on life or 'yes' men/women. You need honest eyes.

If you already have someone who is experienced in this field, their input will be very valuable and this way you can work on areas that you may not be familiar with.

Do I have to show my business plan when I seek bank loans?

Yes, you might have to show your business plan when you seek a bank loan since the bank or any other financial institution will want to know your whole business in detail and get a look at their financial commitment. Preparing a good business plan is the key to getting loan.

Once you develop a good business plan, it can be your guide for whatever new businesses you might want to start in future. The whole idea of a business plan is to get your whole idea on paper, and scan it to detect any flaws and work on it. This is the only way you can find solutions to potential problems in the future and the golden guide to get you out of troubles.

Also, in the future, you may want to sell your business, submitting a business plan will help the buyers get in-depth knowledge about your business and what steps should be taken in future.

CHAPTER 2

BEFORE YOU GET STARTED

Tips and factors to consider and things to remember before you sit down to write your plan. How to think constructively and give your business a frame

Writing a business plan can be quite an overwhelming task. Of course there are many software programs online that can help you with it, but the very fact of putting down your whole idea into few pages can be a bit stressful. Perhaps, you may feel like an author who is about to pen down his entire idea – *"It's all in my head, but every time I sit down to write, nothing happens."*

Well, to be frank, almost every businessman who first started his business has gone through the same phase. As with many things in life, the key to getting started with most difficult things when you are overwhelmed is all about movement.

We agree that writing a business plan is not an easy task, as this single document is as valuable as gold and diamonds. This document is your business's prototype and a reflection of your capability as a businessperson. So under no circumstances do you want it to fall short.

For those who are struggling with their business plan writing, here are some excellent tips complied to bring out the best from you:

Rome Was Not Built In A Day

Rome was not built in a day (neither will your business plan be). Thinking about a business plan, designing its structure, categorizing it, and drafting it all together into some pages will take its time. Don't worry about your business plan being done in a day. You need to take time to think and process your ideas and then put it down. You should not be on "hurry up" mode when you are writing a business plan, because the rush will make you forget, skip and make mistakes that you may regret later. New business owners are under the assumption that they can put down their ideas in less than 48 hours and come up with a masterpiece. This is a wrong assumption. While it is possible to create a business plan in a few days, a good and full-proof plan will take longer. Hence, it's always wise to take your time, spending a week or more going over your writing and coming up with a good and effective business plan.

Why Not Dessert First?

While it may seem to be stress-free to write the easy part first, it makes total sense to do it. Writing what you know first will make it easier for you to get started, and then you will notice that you will start figuring out the rest yourself. The reason why you need to get started with what you know is to get moving, and once you get into the flow or idea, thoughts and plan of action will come automatically. Secondly, seeing your ideas pouring out on paper is a self-stimulus that will help you move on with enthusiasm. Before you know it, you might have created a masterpiece for yourself.

First try 'Brain Dump'

When you get started, your first draft should be a simple 'brain dump'. This means to dump all your ideas randomly on the paper. It's just like when kids dump a box of toys on the floor and then pick up pieces they want to keep. Don't take it as if your first draft will be your final version, because if you do so, you will start getting conscious, and then words won't come out. The idea here is to make your brain feel less conscious and give it more freedom to spit out all that it has in mind. You're brainstorming; so don't worry about simple issues like grammar, sentence structure or style of writing. This way you will have the freedom of writing whatever you like, without going through the pressure of 'finishing' something or correcting something on the spot, which sometimes interrupts thoughts.

Build A Strong Foundation

Writing documents like a business plan can be a difficult task, and just like anything else, a little planning before you write can go a long way. Like a house, your business plan needs a strong foundation on which you can build and develop your ideas. The foundation is the most important part of your business. Build this section really well and then you can slowly work on the other parts that come along afterwards. Some people find it easy to do an outline first and then fill it with their ideas in detail. It's totally okay to try this strategy. Once your outline is complete, concentrate on the important categories and start building the foundation. Once you begin building the foundation, the rest will fall into place.

'Professional' Isn't Always About Sophistication

Many first time business owners feel that if they need to create something 'professional', they need to make it really sophisticated with tough words, sentences and complex ideas. This is not true at all. Always keep your business plan simple and straight, because you need to show this to people and make them understand it. People from all walks of life will be taking a look at your plan, and not everybody will have the 'high intelligence' to understand every bit that's on the paper. Moreover, only you can simplify your business idea and pass on the message to people. Do not assume that whoever takes a look at your document will immediately understand the whole concept. Additionally, keeping your readers awake while reading your document is very important for your success! Hence, KEEP IT SIMPLE.

You Don't Have To Be Right The First Time

As mentioned earlier, don't expect to be absolutely right the first time. Your first draft might not look anything like your final draft. This is absolutely okay. Allow yourself the luxury of committing mistakes, erasing words, producing multiple drafts, each with the sole purpose of creating the perfect piece.

Don't forget that your business plan is not an auto-biography, nor is it a journalistic writing. A business plan is a 'fiction' that is written to explain a 'reality' that you hope to give life to in future. No matter how much you try to create the best plan ever, the end is almost always judicious guessing.

The best part about a business plan is that once you start to reap your benefits of success, the plan will help you guide towards a better and more successful future.

Remember a business plan is not something carved in stone, it's not a scientific explanation, but is a work of art, which is open to be restructured and made more beautiful with time.

QUESTIONS YOU SHOULD CONSIDER BEFORE YOU SIT DOWN TO WRITE

- How will you find your customers? Are you going to call them personally, advertise massively or rely on word of mouth?
- How will you make your product unique? How will you set yourself apart from your competitors?
- How much should you charge for your product or services, such that it makes a profit for you, yet is affordable for your customers?
- How will you deliver your service or product? Are you going to rely on direct sales, use distributors or the internet? How cost effective can you make this?
- How can you ensure utmost customer satisfaction? How can you turn your customers into loyal fans?
- What kind of customer service will you provide in case of an issue?

How To Write A Business Plan

Customer Perspective – The only way that you can make a plan that can be understood by anyone and everyone is to write with from a customer's perspective. As you write, you should list the specific requirements of different audiences. For instance, an investor will only be interested in knowing the financial commitment he/she is getting into. Therefore you need to detail each and every expense. In the same way, a customer will want to know the quality and the price offered. So you should list such requirements clearly.

Market Research – Investors today know the importance of market research and this is exactly why they expect entrepreneurs to come up with a detailed market research. Your plan should include the market size you are going to target, its predicted growth potential and how you can enter into the market. This detailed study will give you and your investor an idea about the need for your business, its potential growth and the kind of local or global problems you might face.

Competitors – As they say – *Keep your friends close, but keep your enemies closer.* From the time you had an idea of starting a business, your first instinctive thought should've been – your competitor! That's right; even your investor wants to know the same. If you need to make anything unique you have to stand apart from your competitor, and the only way to do this is to study your competitor well and strike where they lack. A good business strategy that can out beat your competitor is most important.

Attention to Detail – While writing a business plan we tend to forget the small things or minute tasks in between, but concentrate on the big efforts. Well, small things like a training program for management or your managers to operate a business, or perhaps commuting expenses for your employees, small company funds for any perks or incentives, expense for a coffee machine are small things that can be clearly missed. These things might seem like simple expenses, yet they're important when it comes to operations. So you need to get it covered in your business plan. In other words, sweat the small stuff.

Opportunity – If you are pulling in or trying to attract an investor you need to show him or her the growth opportunity of your business, and how they will benefit from it in the future. How will the investor benefit from investing in your business, compared to investing in some other business or endeavor like stocks or bonds? This is crucial because you want to make the investor totally comfortable in investing in your business.

Do The Math – Your calculations should all be full and accurate. This will include the sales, profit figure, expected income per month and annually, the investment to be put in, the ratio of investment to profit and more. If you are not comfortable with calculations, get someone to help you figure this out. But make sure your calculations are done, as it will remove any uncertainties and assumptions.

Executive Summary – This is the crucial part of every business plan and includes the entire summary of the business idea. This summary is an outline of the whole business plan--in a page or two. This sums up your business idea and cuts through all of the minutia. It is also useful for time pressed investors. This way, an investor can get a quick highlight of the whole business idea, without going through the entire business plan.

Once you finish writing the entire business plan, you should probably have someone review the document. Choose someone who is entirely detached from the process and ask him or her for their honest criticism. This will give you the opportunity to work on something that may raise doubts in the eyes of the investor.

Also, if you sell your business in the future, a business plan will help your buyers to get an in-depth view on your business. They will know where you have started, the position you are in and where your company is being directed. This is very helpful for them, and is stress a free strategy to maintain.

CHAPTER 3
EXECUTIVE SUMMARY

A snapshot of your business plan, your company profile and your goal

An executive summary is one of the most crucial parts of a business plan. It is the first thing that others will read and the last thing that you should be writing. It is nothing but a brief synopsis of your entire business plan. This is written so that people who do not have time to go through the entire document know at a glance what you have in mind and what actions need to be taken.

However, there is a catch. An executive summary is not just a whole summary of your proposal but it is a SALES PITCH that you will be throwing at people with reasons why the customer should be buying from you and how an investor can benefit from your business.

Unfortunately, a lot of people just summarize their business in this executive summary and make it a boring piece of text, which doesn't attract anyone, and hence, is always rejected by investors, banks and customers.

The executive summary should focus on the basic issues, the

demand for your business and the bottom line results. Starting with these simple factors will set the tone of your summary, and then you can follow it up with statistics.

What Does Your Executive Summary Aim To Do?

- Your executive summary aims to be a brief overview of your entire business plan, so that managers and executives can read the document alone without assistance from anyone.
- Allow the reader to quickly understand what's in-store for him/her, before proceeding to read the entire document.
- To be a compelling and persuasive document, so that the reader will feel its value while reading.
- Provide concise, self-supporting, complete and specific information about the business that can be read and comprehended without any external support.

How To Write And Executive Summary

The Problem

Every business is a 'solution' to customer's problem. So the first thing that you should be addressing is your observation of the customer's business requirement, the crisis situation or the lack of supply for a particular demand. You have to define the problem, the need and the goal of the customer's actual requirements. It should reflect your research on the customer's situation and show that you understand their problem and have come up with a solution to it.

For example – If you have researched and found out that there is a $5 million loss in revenue due to a lack of digital records in small time businesses and you have come up with the software or the service to make up for that loss, your 'UNIQUE' product can make money hand over fist.

By doing that, here's what happens. You have directly hit the intended target and have addressed the unique need for it. You have also captured the attention of the reader and now he/she feels that it's worth continuing to read. Creating this curiosity is the best way to hold the attention of the investor and make them buy into your plan.

Outcome

Here, again you describe the potential impact on the customer side if the problem is addressed. You need to show how the need is fulfilled and how the goal is achieved. However, remember, this is not the section that talks about the benefits and features of your product. Instead, it focuses on the company and the profit it is going to make from implementing your business idea.

For instance – When you address problem 1, you will make 50% more profit. Or perhaps, when you achieve goal 2, it will allow you to open up a new market space.

The executive summary should generate a strong feeling in the investor to move forward with your plan. Focusing on addressing the customer need creates the possibility of attention in the reader, and focusing on the payoff will make the investor buy your deal.

Solution

This is the part where you need to put in jargon for the proposed solution to the problem. Typically, each solution that you put forward should focus on solving the customer's problem on one end, and creating profits for you at the same time on the other end. This two-tie solution-profit deal is what will champion your plan.

For instance – We are planning to implement plan A because it can solve customer's problem A, and will generate X% value and profit for the firm.

This is a completely balanced business plan, where the investor knows that he/she is going to win the heart of the customer as well as create profit for his pocket. So you need to know both sides of the game to make the reader interested.

Call of Action

Here is where you directly ask the investor or the reader to participate with you. It can be put as simple as "We would like you to be our investor" or "We are eager to work with you". While asking this, make sure you mention why your business plan is different from others in the market, and what makes your product unique. You need to also show why the person/ investor should invest their money on your business rather than just keeping it the bank or investing in stocks or anything else.

What To Focus On

Try your best to avoid putting in all the cost and expenses in the executive summary unless the investor has specifically demanded that the price be mentioned. Instead, try to focus on compelling the investor by giving your solution to the customer's problems, the uniqueness of your business or project and the gains one can get from implementing your plan.

Sometimes, seeing the huge cost upfront may make the investor go into a defense mode, where he or she will try to question and be indifferent to your plans.

7 Tips to remember while you write your business plan

Avoid Last Minute Writings

Don't wait to do the executive summary writing at the last minute. This is one of the most crucial parts of your business plan; it requires careful thought, consideration and time to develop. If you rush at the last minute, chances are you might skip one or two very important points, you may not be able to put in the right sales pitch, or you will just end up copying something from the Internet.

Although, you might sit down to write your summary, after you have finished the entire business plan document, it is important that you mention every aspect of the business. This can only come if you give yourself the time to think and smartly put it into words. After all, it is this summary that will be approved by investors; so don't treat it like it's a high school or college paper that will constitute 5% of your grade because it's not. You either get it right or you go home.

Look Through the Eyes of Others

Remember when you write your executive summary, you are actually writing for others and not for yourself. This means you need to review your summary from the eyes of the reader. Put in words, terminology and sentences in such a way that the common man or woman can understand.

If your executive summary looks like rocket science, chances are that you will only attract rocket scientists, while the rest of the investors will be investing in others. Not everyone who reads your document has background knowledge of your business, so you need to put in layman's terms and make it a full-proof summary. For instance, if you are a software expert and you write your business plan in the language of complex codes, programs, indexes and highly technical terms, you will be shown the door – without even trying!

Take Your Reader Into Your Dream Word

That's the biggest talent of any salesman. If you need to sell your plan to someone, you need to take him or her and show them the beauty of your dream world. Share your dream, make your document highly compelling like an Academy Award worthy dramatic movie that can keep your readers interested and highly motivated.

If you put down a plan that only you can understand, you are taking your readers to snooze world!

Seeing Is Believing

Ever wondered why magazines have pictures? Why chidden love to flip through magazines? Why magazines are always in demand? Well, it's the pictures in them that speak a thousand words. People believe what they see, and a magazine shows you just that. An article about Harley Davidson may not make an impact on you, but if you throw in a picture in there, you know the difference.

That's right; a picture can make a huge difference, especially for those who don't have good background knowledge about your business. You can simply show them relevant pictures about what you are talking about and those pictures can make a great impact along with your sales pitch.

Do Not 'JUNK' It

Do not go on and on about your executive summary and make it as long as your entire document. Use words as if they are golden. This means, you need to keep a word limit for the entire summary. This is the only way that you can cut out the 'junk' and concentrate on what's more important. You will also choose words carefully and will make it the best piece possible.

Otherwise, if you allow yourself the luxury of writing page after page after page after page, you are negating the entire premise of a 'summary'.

Do A Selected Review

Sometimes we are so liberal that we involve everyone around us to assist in writing the executive summary. This is great and a very fair policy, this way, no one should be able to blame you later that they were not involved in the making of this huge business idea. But the negative side of this huge involvement is that you get so many different opinions and views that you may miss the point.

Different people have different perceptions and different ideas on how and which direction a document should be written. If you listen to everyone out there, chances are that you may end up with something totally different from your original idea of the plan.

Keep It Simple

A lot of summaries start with a long narrative about the business background and structure. This instantly bores the reader. Try to grab the reader from the beginning itself. If you have to use movie script like writing, do it. But it shouldn't be boring at all. This is a skill only you can create, and no one else can make it up for you. Remember, it's your plan, and you need to get it registered in the mind of your investor by hook or crook.

Do not complicate things and throw ideas that needs time to think and understand. Simplicity always works when it comes to making someone understand something. As mentioned earlier, do not use too many technical terms and complex language, because the idea here is to convey the message and not judge your writing skills.

If you feel that you are not too good at writing, hire someone who is. That's right; take help from someone who can write a compelling text for you. This will not stop you from planning the narrative and putting in all the messages. It's only the writing skills that you are borrowing.

CHAPTER 4

COMPANY DESCRIPTION

Providing information on what you do, how you are different from your competitors and the target audience you want to serve.

The company description is the second section of your business plan. It comes after the Executive summary, and is ideally an opening point of your business plan. The company description covers all the important details about the company, its core business, the employees, the location, your proposed business idea and your future goals.

It also focuses on the vision and direction it plans to follow and is the general framework to show how your professional platform operates. This is the place where you need to create an impression on your readers and investor.

Also known as the company profile, this section is the point where your investors will get to know the size of your business/company, your vision and the way you plan to lead your business.

What should be included in a Company description?

Basic Information

- Nature of business – the first and foremost point to be mentioned in your company description is the type of industry you belong to and what you might be offering as a product or services in the industry
- Structure – You should mention the legal structure of the company and also mention why you have chosen such a structure. Try to mention how the structure works for your business needs.
- Mission – Not quite required at this stage, but it would be okay if you had a mission to follow. This can be 30 to 40 words which encompasses your guiding values and principles.

Objective and Goals

- Objectives – this is what you wish to achieve and what can be measured. For instance, your objective can be to increase the sales value by 50% within the next 12 months.
- Goals – This is where you want to reach into the future and describe how your goal can be reached within your objective. For example, if your objective is to increase sales by 50% in the next 12 months, your goal will be to generate twice the profit and develop the business in the next 3 years.

Target Market

Every business has a target audience, if you don't, then you don't have a unique product. This is the very reason why you need to have a target audience listed in your company description. Your target audience will be your customers based on their age, job role, income and more.

It will also include how you plan to reach your target audience and how you plan to expand in the future.

Resources

Describe your business as well as your industry along with its size and any future growth. Also, list the future predicted demand for your product or service. Then, include how many resources, or employees you are planning to bring into the company along with their skill(s) and experience. Each resource that you list should show significant importance of how it contributes to the growth of your company and its business.

How to Write a Company Description

- Study – No one has a born skill to readily and effortlessly write a company description, especially if you are writing a business plan to start up new business. So the first and the best thing to do is to study your competitor and other companies that are in your industry and that conduct the same nature of business. Notice the style of writing they use when they describe their company. Take notes on words, sentences and phrases that grab attention of the readers and make your writing more interesting.
- Uniqueness – When you list the nature of your business, its values, purpose, mission and other such factors, make sure that you write how your business is unique and how it stands apart from your competitors. Your business profile should convey the personality and style of your business and this will help you set the tone of your business plan.
- Industry – Mention what kind of industry your company will belong to. The characteristics of such an industry. This will give the reader the entire view of your business,

and the message you want to convey. For example, if you are a start-up, you will concentrate on the profit your business will make in the industry. If your company has been operating for a long time, your history is your main strength, while high tech companies will focus more on the technical skills and the growth potential of the business.

- Products and Services – Here's the catch, especially if you are trying to get an investor to be involved in your start-up company. The type of product or service you offer has a lot to do in the way your company will function, its growth potential and its market presence. Make sure you have something unique to offer.
- Simple Language – Make sure whatever you write, you write it in layman's terms. Do not use too many technical jargons and make the whole thing complicated and difficult for your investor to read. Remember not everybody will have the background and technical knowledge of your business and its industry.
- Address – Include the full address and location of your company space. If you are going online, make sure your company maps well in Google maps and other such navigation systems.
- Consumers – Make sure you give a detailed study on the type of customers you are targeting. Although this will be mentioned in the target audience section, this section will have details about the customer's demands and problems and the services you will be introducing to solve these problems.
- Competitive Advantage – Explain the advantage your company has over your competitors in terms of your products, services, pricing, efficient operations, expert employee structure or any other abilities that bring value to the company.

Factors to Consider When Writing a Company Description

Elevator Pitch

Always start your company description in such a way that it captures the attention of the readers. Use an elevator pitch strategy when it comes to your company and express any key characters that make it stand apart from the crowd. This is highly important because your opening line needs to get hold of your reader's imagination.

Big Picture Frame

Instead of including every small detail in each section of your description, try to keep an overview phase in the entire segment. You can save the details for later in the related sections of the document. The big picture frame will not bore your readers; it will give all the necessary information.

Passion

Your passion can be very well reflected in the company description section. If you have rushed with your description, chances are that it will show in the writings as well. Let your passion roll out in this section of your business plan, as the writing will have a passionate tone and will make the reader interested in your idea.

Keep it Short

This is only the company description and no one is expecting you to write an entire story about your company. Always keep a length check and restrict it to a certain amount of words. Sometimes, when you include your passion and excitement into your writing, you might get carried away, and this will lead to a boring and long company description.

Proofread

Make sure you do not make any spelling or grammatically errors in this section because this might be viewed as carelessness and can turn off potential investors. However, if you have a great idea or a great business, wise investors won't think twice about it, but still, make sure you proofread your entire document once you've finished writing it.

Also, a great company profile should not limit itself with products and services, but a little personality infused in it can go a long way. A little business culture with a personal touch can make it a bit more personalized, which can resonate with the reader.

In addition, adding information about the company's support to humanity and societal issues in general can be easily identified and brings more value to the document. A human perspective to the section and explanation of how profits and business can help people to live a better life and do less harm to the community and environment can increase the value of your business as well as your company.

CHAPTER 5
MARKET ANALYSIS

Before you put your business out there you need to have a perfect idea on the type of market that exists and which market should be penetrated. A good study of your competitors gives you a basic idea on the potential of your business success

The most important part of any business plan is the market research. Before you can roll out your business strategies, products, services, and sales potential, you need to first figure out your market and what should be done to fulfill any demand. Based on the market research you can successfully build a marketing plan and an implementation strategy.

Starting a business without a market research is like firing into open air without any target in mind – you will never achieve anything!

Market Research- What is it?

A market is a place where goods can be sold to a particular class of people or to a particular place. A market research is usually conducted to know the potential sale of a particular product or service in a specific market. Every business needs to have buyers to whom they can sell their product. If you don't know if there are buyers out there, how in the world can you produce anything?

It is simply foolish to make a business decision based on your 'gut feeling' or a hunch. Market research is a more accurate way of finding out whether your business will survive in the market. You can either hire a marketing agency that can conduct the research for you, or you can do it yourself.

Different Types Of Market Research:

Primary Market Research

Whenever you approach someone directly, that is, talk to competitors, customers, you are gathering primary research information. This is also known as qualitative market research. This is usually the most valuable and credible research for your business. You can call people personally and interview them or ask them their opinions about the demand for a product that you would like to sell. Based on several replies you can rely upon statistics or a probability ratio of its potential sale.

Secondary Market Research

This is a research which will be done by other people or organizations for you. This is an indirect approach of gathering relevant information about your market. This type of research can be less accurate when compared to primary research, but is still a crucial basis to make your analysis. It is cost effective and gives you a general perception of market trends.

Sources Of Secondary Market Research Include:

- Libraries
- Private Research Companies
- Regional or City councils
- Internet

- Trade Organizations
- Chamber of Commerce
- Government Companies and Departments

Categories Involved In A Market Research

Specific Market Research

This is gathering information for a specific problem. For instance, if you have a question like, "How much will people pay for a cup of coffee?" It is important to describe your industry including its current size, its potential growth, its historic growth as well as other characteristics and trends like projected growth rate, different phases etc. you could also mention important customer groups within your industry so that you can be specific.

Manageable Target Audience

You need to analyze and narrow down your target audience to a manageable size. This is where most businesses go wrong because they try to impress too many target audiences, which gets them confused and ultimately leads to failure. Knowing who your target audience is and narrowing down in size is the only way that you can come to concrete figures.

Separate characteristics

Once you narrow down the size of your target audience you need to critically analyze the basic needs of your potential customers. You need to answer questions like; are these needs being met? What are the demographics of the group(s) mentioned and where are they located? Are there any prevailing cycle or seasonal purchasing trends that create a great impact on your business as well as your target audience? This is identifying the basic need of your target audience.

The Size Of Your Core Target Market

Apart from identifying the size of your target market, what statistics can you present regarding the annual purchase of your market and the revenue in your industry? What is the predicted market growth of this particular target audience? This is all about making a market profile where you see the fluctuations of your target audience's purchasing trends and more. This is more like a study to know if your product will remain in the market and the life span it has.

How much market presence can you gain? Your market share percentage and the size of customers you expect to purchase your products in a defined location. You need to also put down the logic behind your estimation because; your estimation is a contributing factor in terms of geographical patterns, purchasing trends, customer attributes and more.

Pricing Of Your Products As Well As The Gross Margin Target - you need to put down why you have decided on a particular pricing structure, the gross margin level, and any promotional discounts that you plan to use in the future. If you are including any kind of research study or getting market tests done, make sure that you concentrate on the results of these tests. Any additional information should go in the appendix.

Competitive Analysis - this is the part where you need to identify who your competition is in terms of your product or service and their market segmentation. You need to rate your competition on the following:

- How much of the market share they have
- Any strength or weakness that they have
- The importance of your target audience to your competitors

- Where you find the opportunity to enter the market
- Do you find any barriers that may stop you from entering the market
- Are there any indirect competitors that are affecting your success
- What kind of barriers do you see in the market

Any Legal Restrictions - You need to include any government or customer regulation requirements that may affect the implementation or success of your business and how you are planning to overcome it. If it involves any kind of expense you need to put it down in your analysis.

DIY Market Research

If you are planning to start up your first business, chances are that you might not have enough financial capability to hire a professional market research company to do this part of your business plan. So what do you do? You do it yourself!

Although you might not have a great idea about your market, you can research on the Internet a profile of your customer type, the kind of competitors you have and their products, should give you enough data to create an impact in your business plan writing.

Internet

One of the easiest and convenient ways to doing your part of market research in the comfort of your home is to research on the Internet. If you know your direct competitor, go to their site and study them, do some research on their products or services mentioned AND on other people's website as well.

Product availability is a very important factor in your business plan. So you need to make sure if your products can be ordered online and by any other outlets that you desire.

Outdoor

The next step would be to go outdoors and hire a mystery shopper. You can be a mystery shopper yourself since there is no greater way of analyzing your competition or their services but by approaching them directly.

Businesses like catering and restaurants need to directly check out their rival establishment. If your name is well known, ask your friend to go for a meal and get to know things through him or her. You need to find out if the food is good, is there any special wine listed? Does there service match or compare to industry standards? What's your competitor's USP (Unique Selling Point)? Are you able to match them or bring better services?

If you do your market research perfectly, you will be getting enough or more information to organize your business such that you get better advantage over your rival.

You can do your spy work and go to your rival's establishment and check out their premises and how they function. You need to see how attractively their products are placed or how accessible their products are. Also, are there any items that do not sell?

Sometimes the location plays a very important role in the success or failure of a business. Even product placement in a retail store can affect its sales.

Market research is all about understanding the potential sale of your product in a particular market. The moment you begin to figure this out, everything else will fall in place and you will be able to compile a good market analysis of your own.

CHAPTER 6

MANAGEMENT AND ORGANIZATION

An organization's management structure is its operating manual. Without an operating manual, there is no way to make an organization function, either in a good way or a bad way. Believe it or not, even a poorly functioning organization has some sort of operating manual, even if it is coming from the instincts of its key people who run the business. These organizations function poorly because their management structure is nowhere near foolproof.

The best advantage a structure affords you is that every member in an organisation is expected to perform certain responsibilities and tasks that are clearly outlined in the organization's manual. There is no confusion or space for argument on who is supposed to perform a specific task. With organizational growth, the tasks and responsibilities that were unforeseen before makes its entry into the organization and this is when you will have problems reallocating the tasks to various individuals.

A management structure is significant for a company in today's world because unlike the organizations that were founded before the 20th century that were typically family owned and run businesses, today's companies aspire to grow internationally and in order to achieve successful global exchanges, it is imperative to have a proper business structure.

Four Key Benefits of Organizational Structure

1. Clear guidelines on how to proceed – When each member is clear about his or her tasks and responsibilities within the organization, there is very little space for confusion. This keeps the organization running without any problems.
2. Better connection between members and employees – Sometimes, the feeling of being overworked comes to a person's mind simply because his/her tasks were not clearly described properly to him/her from the beginning.
3. The lifeline – There are scarcely any organizations that are run without an organizational structure or in other words, it's the lifeline of an organization. Of course, you can run something without a manual if you are highly experienced but passing off a company to your descendants is not going to be an easy task without it.
4. Track Progress – If there is one way to track the performance of each individual, it is organization structure. In large companies, they employ performance reports to do so. This enhances organizational structure significantly.

The right time to work on your Organizational Structure

An organizational structure is very important in a company or business and it is recommended to create one in the early stages of the company's formation. This is particularly important if you are going for venture capitalist funding or any form of outside investment, because an investor is least likely to spend their money on a firm that does not have any idea on the tasks and responsibilities of its members.

The problem with many companies, especially start-ups or those going through a financial loss is that they have important things to take care of and it sometimes requires going beyond your specified tasks. However, there are also chances that some people will work much harder than others. To create a balance, you need a clear structure.

Key Elements Of Organizational Structure

1: Governance

Who is going to make the decisions for the organization? Who is going to sign off on important business documents? Who will have the authority to take care of unforeseen circumstances? Who will be the company's spokesperson to the press and to what extent can he or she disclose key decisions? These are just some of the aspects that governance in an organization covers but there is more to it, such as making important financial decisions that steers the company clear of trouble.

2: Work Distribution

In the beginning of a company's life, there will be a few people that get things started. This is the very group that plans the entire running of the company with the available funds, looking for resources for more funds and the development of the company with growing needs.

The executive committee makes key decisions on necessary changes in the board and strategic changes in accordance with the various circumstances that a company has to go through in its growth.

Task forces are created for a company to expand its business horizon by launching their products as planned, launching new products or expanding their range. An action committee decides on necessary changes that are required to change the company's wellbeing. If you don't have one, you might have to start with yourself.

3: Marketing

You need a marketing team to market your product. If you cannot afford one, you very well may have to start with you.

4: Business Development

Without new business being developed from time to time, you will not be able expand your company. This is why you need a business development team.

We will discuss marketing and business development in detail later.

The Basic Business Structure

There are four types of business forms. They include, proprietorship, partnership, corporation and S Corporation. There is Limited Liability Company (LLC) and Limited Liability Partnership (LLP). Your decision to choose a business model depends on the tax structure of government for your form of business, your expansion plans and partnership deals are some factors that will help you in deciding the right business structure.

Your business structure has a significant impact on the management structure because if you are running a sole proprietorship, it means you are the very individual that owns the enterprise. You may, however, need employees to ship your items and market your products so even a sole proprietorship needs a good business plan.

THE BASICS OF COMPANY BUSINESS STRUCTURE

1: Board Of Directors

The first step of any company is the board of directors. In large corporations, shareholders elect members. Board of Directors select CEO's, CFO's, mangers, presidents or other key roles that they and the shareholders find appropriate. They can dismiss them as well. However, board of directors are not significant for a start-up as long as the company does not require massive structure and investment.

2: Management Team

The typical management team consists of a CEO (Chief Executive Officer), who is the top manager who is responsible for a company's operations. He reports to the chairman and board of directors but in modern start-ups, people hold the responsibility of a CEO at the time of being on the board. Then there is the COO or Chief Operations Officer, who runs the operations in a company such as the sales, production, marketing and business development. A CFO or Chief Financial Officer reports to the CEO and his job is to analyze the financial data.

3: The Style Of Administration

Different companies have different administration styles. Most start-ups in today's ecommerce world are more casual in terms of addressing superiors, dress code and the overall mannerisms in the workplace where in older companies; they tend to be more formal. Your management structure should decide what approach you want to take.

41

4: Industry Analysis

Industry analysis is performed to position your company and see the difference between you and larger companies so that you can outline the necessary changes in the management plan that can accommodate the changes that comes with the company's growth.

Conclusion

You can refer to the sample business plan (Which is right before the Grant Writing portion of this book) to get an idea of a business management plan. Just remember that your key people can only create a business management plan for a company because what works for one company may not be suitable for someone else's. Moreover, the way you want to manage your enterprise may be totally different from someone else that has different points of views about the whole process.

In a nutshell, you can conclude that there is no standardized way to run a company and this is the key challenge in wiring a management plan. Keep one thing in mind: do not be overoptimistic about the tasks and responsibilities you can perform. Owners tend to do this in order to cut the costs but this is not always a smart idea. Sometimes you have to spend those dollars where it's needed to run your company the way it deserves to be run to get the best result you desire.

CHAPTER 7

YOUR BUSINESS PRODUCT

This is the most important chapter in this book. Your product or service is the most important part of your business plan. After all, what is a business plan without a product or service? Your product or service is your business. But, understanding the concept of product or service is more complex than creating a product and placing it in the market. There are many important things that make your business plan click.

If your company is unknown to the consumer market, you will have to first establish how your company is different from others and the advantages of using your company's products over the competition. However, a product position strategy in a business plan has to pay attention to the many other aspects including:

1: The Design

In an internal company discussion, you will not pay much attention to the design because your effort will be spent more on getting the product created and making sure it is good. However, in order to attract potential investors and good employees, you need to convince them that you have something to sell. It goes without saying that the quality of your product and other factors are the key in selling it but what is the single most important thing in creating the necessary attraction with your product? It is the visual appeal or design… the X Factor.

Even if it is a service, the designing principles can go a long way in creating a convincing service. Some of the key aspects that are considered in the design are:

- The packaging – The product needs to have an interesting package to create value.
- Web Design – Even the best of products with a crappy looking website will have a tough time convincing your company's brand image.

2: Product Position

Why is your product different from others? Let's say you are selling organic tomatoes: you certainly aren't the first person to do so and you won't be the last one either. So it is imperative to convince your buyers that your tomatoes are different than others. Now, this can be done in different ways:

- Suggesting unique farming techniques
- Talking about sustainable agricultural practices in your farm
- The price factor (yours is the cheapest organic brand or your tomatoes maybe a little high on the price front but it comes with undefeatable quality)
- The quality factor

Organic tomatoes are a necessary vegetable in many households and the selling part can be really easy when compared to an ecommerce store that sells handmade jewellery. However, each one has its own merits and this can be explored completely with the help of product positioning.

3: The 'This product is created for you' Approach

In the mass market, sending a personal message to customers that buy toothpaste has very little impact when compared to a wedding photographer that addresses the typical problems and solutions of new brides and grooms' in his proximity. With this approach, the wedding photographer convinces his prospects that he understands exactly what new brides and grooms' want, need and require in order for the experience of their special day to be captured for a lifetime. This will attract more customers to him because the customer will develop the feeling that the photographer already knows what they want.

Interestingly, the quality of a service and product is a second concern if the product is positioned carefully. There, of course, shouldn't be any discrepancies in a product's claimed quality and the actual product because it will attract negative reviews and after the initial interest in your company, people will move on and some of them will even have negative reviews.

4: The Market

Some products are hard to sell because there is no market for them or because the market for the specific product is inaccessible. Let's say you found out that charcoal grills can sell like hot-cakes in Australia but you live in the USA. You can still ship a product to Australia but if the shipping costs are very high and you have to setup your establishment in Australia, and you will have to rework and retool your entire business plan.

So yes, your product needs a market that is accessible and profitable and not overcrowded. For example, there are tons of Internet marketing businesses that require minimal setup and experience from the starter. Due to the increased flexibility of starting up an internet marketing business, hundreds of people are starting this new business model each year and penetrating the market has become really difficult, if not impossible.

5: The Margin

Once you workout your investment and operational costs, you need to set a breakeven point timeframe so that you can determine when your company starts making profits. But understand that the return of investment (ROI) can't be set for a specific time period. For example, if you are competing in a highly competitive niche and your equipment costs are very high, you may simply wait longer to break even wherein a service can break even in the first year itself. Some small start-ups might become profitable after two or three months because the investment costs are slight.

These 5 things determine if your product is a worthy investment. You of course won't start a company with something that is not worthy of selling but the margin will give you an exact idea about the foreseeable challenges and what you can do about it.

6: Market Research

Understand, that although your product has a market, it's not enough to create a product and attempt to sell it to that market. Sometimes, your market's purchasing power and their willingness to spend a specific amount on your product are the only two keys that may connect them to your product. That's why many business owners prefer to sell products that consumers need rather than what they don't need. Unless you grab a your wrinkled clothes out of a pile each day and throw them in another pile when you get ready for bed, you need hangers. Although it might be great to have one, you don't really need a 60 inch Full 3D Flat screen TV.

Market research will help you determine who will be inclined to buy your product, based on past purchases, income level, age, gender, where they live, etc. It will also allow you to locate your competitors, discover your competitive advantage (if there is any) and the size of the market.

7: Your Competition

Understanding your competition is very important. It will give you an idea about the price point and also their plans for the market. If you and they have more than one product, what's their biggest seller? What colours do customers prefer? What's their inventory? Do they have inventory? You can learn a lot from your competition. If the competition has priced their products at a costly amount- that does not mean that you should be tempted to launch yours at a ridiculously low rate. A slight price differential is enough.

Once your product is positioned in the right manner, there is no way your competition can beat your presence. However, in order to beat your competition and get the leading market share, you will have to work harder and smarter. And understand this, whenever you are able to penetrate the market, it will be difficult to go beyond that initial level of growth, unless you have branding strategies and marketing. Reaching the top position is not possible without paying attention to launching your product the right way.

CHAPTER 8

MARKETING YOUR PRODUCT

Why would your business plan include a marketing plan for your product? Well, there are two reasons:

- First, your investor will get an idea about the marketing plan you have in mind and see how attractive it is.
- Secondly, a marketing plan is often a reflection of the actual money that you can spend on the operational and business developmental costs.

The first step in marketing your product is creating a sales plan that your investors will like. The first step in marketing is setting sales goals: let's say that you are hitting the market for the first time and your brand is an unknown one: selling 50 units in the first month is a realistic goal.

If it's an expensive product like a washing machine, you may look for a smaller target. This is the smartest way to monitor the progress of your company and see how close you are to reaching your sales goals.

BUILD YOUR INTERNET MARKETING PLAN

New companies can benefit greatly from internet marketing

because internet marketing is inexpensive and reaches a massive audience with the right campaign. As long as your product is targeted at a nationwide traditional customer base, you do not need to rely heavily on traditional modes of advertisements such as newspapers and television.

An Internet marketing plan is very simple and does not require a lot of expertise. If you have issues in creating an online marketing plan, you can seek the help of an online marketing consultant:

- Build Your Keyword List – building your keyword list can't be done without understanding your market and targeting them with the keywords that can create the highest possible impact. Keyword research is a great approach to understand the level of competition for your product or service. If you are offering something that already exists in the market, you will have a tough time getting started.
- Customer Engagement – social media marketing or marketing through Facebook, Twitter and similar social media platforms is not mere marketing but your success comes when the users show an interest in what you are selling. If you can't create this interest, you are not going to position yourself well in the social media segment.
- Don't be that perfect provider – one of the biggest mistakes that many new marketers do is they try offering solutions to all the problems and to every customer. Even if your product has a potential of solving many unforeseen problems, it's not a smart idea to make all these claims. How many of us will buy a shower gel that works as a shampoo and hand wash too? We prefer our shampoos for shampoo and hand wash for hand wash; not an all-in-one solution. Come up with a

simple solution to a single problem and associate with a few small issues that are related to the main problem which can be solved with your product.

An online marketing campaign can yield the perfect result with proper management and targeting specific keywords. The good thing about online marketing is that you can have an average budget and get response results figured out as soon as you get started. It is much easier to tweak your campaign regularly to yield better results.

Online marketing campaigns can expose your products to unknown horizons and make your products socially acceptable. If Amazon was launched as a regular brick and mortar store competing against Wal-Mart, its success today would more than likely be lesser or it may not have succeeded at all. Social media campaigns can also create large audiences with a personal touch that loves your products.

General rules of marketing your product

Do not waste your time achieving perfection

One of the common issues with launching a new product or service is trying to please everyone with every feature. It would be great to squeeze in everything that every potential customer wants but this is impossible for a product or service. You look at any new Smartphone or application launched into the market (the very successful ones): you will find absolutely nothing wrong with them and sometimes wonder if you can actually 'use up' the product due to it's high number of features.

Perfection is a misconception because by the time we achieve something close to perfection, a new technology will emerge that can make things better. That's why we don't have a perfect car or perfect Smartphone. If you think you are going to be the first one to offer a perfect product, you are terribly wrong. However, this doesn't mean you can get away with a junk product either. You need something really good but do not waste your time on achieving perfection.

Spend time testing your product

Keep this very important thought in mind: when you are introducing your product to an investor, the first and foremost thing that the investor will look for are potholes and pitfalls. The same can be expected from customers as well. Your product launch is not going to be like the new iPhone launch or Kindle launch because these are two very good examples of products that created an authority symbol image for themselves in the market.

Preparing for the unexpected

So what if you came up with a product that is substantially unique and can tap a potential market with massive profit? You can sell it for years and see your dream coming true, right? Well, this is not always true: sometimes, an intelligent competitor will duplicate your product within a few months without giving you a chance of filing an infringement suit and introduce it to the market as well. Sometimes, the customer response is not as you expected or the marketing and operational costs will go beyond what you anticipated. These are only some of the examples of the unexpected taking place within your business.

Take Feedbacks Seriously

Marketing is not always converted into a successful sale. Each campaign is targeted to get response from some interested prospects but this doesn't mean you will make a sale each time. There are many reasons for a sale to skip: you couldn't convince your prospects about your product, the prospects can't afford it or it is not serving a purpose.

If you take feedback like these seriously instead of ignoring them, you will find many constructive ways to change your product and marketing plan to address the various concerns of people.

Looking For External Help

You can't create a marketing plan alone. If you create a marketing plan alone, chances are that it's not perfect. Get some expert help, even if it costs you because this is the only way to maintain a foolproof approach with your marketing plan and achieve the results.

How Successful Marketers do it Differently

Understanding the ways of successful Internet marketers is the perfect way to get an idea of tweaking your marketing plan to make it appealing to the mass audience. According to a survey conducted by the state of marketing in 2013, at least 76% of the successful marketers directly interact with their customers every once in a while to see the customer response themselves.

Secondly they train their marketing team. When you launch a new product, you may want to do this differently. If you have less experience, you should consider getting help from a trained professional.

Leading marketers, more than 80% of them at least, use collaboration tools and brand awareness strategies to succeed with their campaign.

Learning from successful people is very important to succeed with a marketing campaign because the marketing plan is the key in getting the anticipated results from your product. Consider doing as much tweaking, as you need to get the best plan you can.

CHAPTER 9

FUNDING YOUR BUSINESS

The term 'funding' is very simple and its meaning is quite obvious: you need money to run a business and it should be sourced from one or multiple channels. In a nutshell, below are the funding options you have:

1. Your savings
2. Family and friends
3. Grants
4. Loans
5. Various forms of debt
6. Venture capitalists

It goes without saying that you can add many more categories and the number can go above 10 easily. However, let's stick to the basics and see the pros and cons of each funding method because the working principle for each funding method is different but these 6 options determine the basic difference between each approach:

Your Savings

The single most advantage of using your savings to start a business is the absolute control over your funds and the freedom to make your own decisions when it comes to how to spend the funds in your favour. However, the downside of funding your own business is the availability (or lack there of) of funds. Most people are less likely to have this kind of money and may require external help.

Family and Friends

The good thing about family and friends is that the borrowing terms are the most flexible other than your own money. However, borrowing money from your closest ones can sour a good relationship and particularly if things go wrong or don't progress as you expected. Sometimes your family and friends may give you suggestions that they find constructive but you find them unworthy. Such interference can also result in harming your relationship.

The Reality of Your Savings & Your Friends and Family

If you have your own money to fund a business, this is the best way to get started but the risk associated with this approach is not small. If the business goes wrong, your lifetime's savings can go down the drain with it and you will end up starting from scratch. This is more than discouraging for most of us and although the saying, "I built it before, I'll build it again." Is true, the second start may not be an easy task.

Borrowing money is a risky proposition when the lender is a friend or family member because you might have trouble paying it back and often times it can take your relationship in the wrong direction. Sometimes pooling the kind of cash required for your business from family or friends is simply not possible.

It is important to clarify whether the money is a loan or investment. If a payback rate is not negotiated, you should add this to the repaid amount.

Special Program Grants

Grants are very good funding options for businesses because when you get approved for grants, you can get more funds through loans. However the grant scene for businesses are highly competitive and getting approved is not easy. Moreover, working on a proposal and getting approved is a time consuming process.

Grants are generally best for non-profit organizations. If you have a non-profit organization, by all means, go for it. There are tons of wealthy individuals and corporations that are interested in giving to various causes. You can refer to the second part of the book for information on Grant Writing for non-profits.

Loans

Loans will give you absolute control over your business and there is a fixed interest rate to pay back the borrowed money. Loans are very flexible and do not leave you in unnecessary financial stress. However, particularly if the economy is bad, loans are also hard to come by, especially for those with a bad credit history. If you do not have any asset(s) to offer as the guarantee for your loan, it is very difficult to get approved for one.

Credit Cards

If you have an approved credit card, this part is very simple. You buy everything through the credit card and get your business started. It goes without saying that the biggest downsides of credit cards usage are the high interest rates. If your business doesn't flourish as you expected, you will be left with several thousands of dollars in debt and paying this money back can be a true burden and may take several years. With credit cards, there is a good chance that you will mix your personal and business expenses together and this can lead to great trouble.

In a nutshell

These funding methods are only suitable for smaller investments. If your business requires a small investment, you can consider these options. However the risks associated with these funding models are very high except for bank loans. Even with bank loans, you are likely to lose some of your valuable assets if your business does not grow as you expected.

ANGEL INVESTORS AND VENTURE CAPITALISTS

Angel investors are typically entrepreneurs or wealthy individuals that want to invest in new talent and get some financial benefits out of it. Angle investment means you are at the lowest risk because you will get sufficient flow of funds in a span of a few years to run your business smoothly. Angel investors are connected with several well connected people in the industry and this connection will help you to grow faster. Sometimes, they can actually bring in customers for your start-up.

The best thing about an angel investment is the possibility of getting help from someone experienced in running a business. Running a business has only a little to do with your product. The marketing, sales, team management and getting whole process rolling is a major thing and many newcomers fail at those tasks.

Venture Capitalists

Venture capitalists are likelier to invest large amounts of cash so that the company can grow faster and reach its targets in shorter periods. When you get your funds approved from a reliable venture capitalist firm or an angel investor, your company's credibility goes up.

With an angel investor and venture capitalist, you do not have full control over your company despite coming up with the product, but you can benefit from their involvement in setting benchmarks and selling your product to a bigger audience and at a better price. However, getting approved for a venture capitalist fund is difficult without a good business plan and proposal and more importantly, having some form of friendship or relationship with either a venture capitalist group or someone who can refer you to them.

CHAPTER 10

CORE ADVANTAGES OF YOUR BUSINESS

The success of every business mostly depends on its uniqueness. What makes your business unique and how can it stand out from the crowd. Here are a few tips on how your business can gain advantages over your competitors in different areas.

If you're writing a business proposal to get an investor, the only thing he would be interested in is the core advantages of your business compared to your rival(s). If you are a start up, you might have to imagine and/or explain how your particular product or service can out perform its rivals in your area, nationally and/or worldwide.

A business will sell or make profits only when it is unique. Everyone wants to hear a unique business idea and if you are writing a business plan, you need to make sure that you point out your advantages over your rivals.

How Do You Do This?

There are standardized categories that you can point your advantages over your rivals. Here are few:

Leadership Advantage

The leadership of your business progress can be made successful by a range of specific activities. They include:

- How you provide targeted mentoring support
- Identifying your present and anticipated business priorities
- How you define and deliver sincere leadership behavior
- How you will drive your business team to their full potential
- How you bring authentic business leadership
- What your vision and priorities are for your business
- Your leadership team encourages feedback and is ready to embrace it

Sustainable Planning Advantage

There was a time when strategic planning was done by only the largest companies. However, times have changed and today it is a simple requirement for every business to survive. Anyone who is leading a business is on a constant watch, anticipating changes and developing new strategies to proactively lead his way to success into the global marketplace.

Without sustainable planning, a business can simply drift along on a non-specific course and may not be able to stand the pressure of the cutthroat competition. Creating a strategy plan can be done for various reasons like efficiency in energy, time, commitment and more experience. Creating a strategy plan is all about realizing and accepting the fact that yesterday's success may not work as a principal guideline for the future.

A Sustainable Business Plan Can Be Created By Keeping These Areas In Mind:

- The overall business health
- Creating new ideas for future success
- Critically analyzing brand strategy, positioning and the effectiveness of the brand
- Identifying the strongest source of profit and revenue potential

Questions That You Need To Ask Yourself When Considering A Sustainable Business Plan

- What is the kind of business you are doing and what is its core purpose?
- How can your company stand out differently from your competitor and how sustainable can you make this practice?
- How can you describe your company's advantage in 45 words or less?
- What is the one factor that is stopping your company from achieving its key goal in the next three years? What are you going to do about it?
- How are you tracking your key performance statistics?

Motivated Employee Advantage:

Getting people to do their best at work even when they are in trying circumstances is one of the most enduring and toughest challenges. Deciphering the key to motivate human beings is a century old puzzle. While philosophers point towards human behavior and psychology, companies today are striving hard to break down this puzzle and bring out the best in their employees.

Fortunately, the new research in fields like biology, newer sciences and evolutionary psychology has allowed humans to peek under the hood and learn more about the human brain and its impact on different communication methods.

Getting every employee to like his or her company and their work is quite a challenging task. However, the incredible benefits of motivated employees leads a company to increase the productivity of work, reduces cost of operations, leads to achievement of organizational goals, builds up a healthy work culture and leads to stability in workforce.

While Calculating Your Motivated Employee Advantage, The Areas Which Can Be Included Are:

- Critically analyzing organizational culture
- Judging employee engagement
- Developing a change in management program
- Creating sincere leadership
- Creating an effective employee structure
- Identifying any key development skills that need to be implemented
- Improving presentation skills

Some Questions You should ask yourself while writing down these advantages are:

- What are the core values of the company? Can any randomly selected employee answer the same questions?
- How successful have you been in embedding its core values?
- How does your company celebrate its success? How does the company handle any disappointment or failure?
- How much are you committed in developing your employee and management skills?

- What should be done so that your employee can describe your company as "an awesome place to work?"

Enhanced Customer Satisfaction Advantage

Achieving high customer satisfaction is the major goal of any business. It takes a lot of business effort to achieve this objective and most businesses spend a significant part of their marketing budget in customer satisfaction surveys. The advantage of business gets from customer satisfaction is hard to overestimate, since they are grouped into four categories - advertising savings, business intelligence, customer retention and pricing strategy. Any business would vouch to the fact that the expense to serve an existing customer is far less than acquiring a new customer. An established customer is already aware of the business and does not need further convincing. However, a new customer needs all that it takes to buy the product and become loyal to the brand.

A satisfied customer means repeated business, more profit, word-of-mouth advertising, positive company image and prospective growth of the business. Unfortunately, consumers are often the first people to know any new competition that your business might have, any new preferences your rival may bring to the market and the latest technological advancements. This can be a threat to your products and services and keeping a customer loyal to your products amidst the tempting and alluring competitor advantage is the success of your business.

Companies today spend a large amount of money on customer satisfaction surveys, because this feedback can make or break the success of a company. It is said that about 20%

of the annual growth of a business can be contribute from careful surveying of existing customers. Customer satisfaction can bring you explosive growth rates, provided that you invest in multiple advertising and promotion efforts to bring in new customers.

Customer Satisfaction Research is a form of research, where you indulge in asking your customers for their feedback regarding your company and its products. A *Customer Satisfaction Research* survey is considered to be a valuable tool for businesses small or large, helping them to gain better understanding on how their customers perceive their company and its products. By monitoring your customer's satisfaction and responding to any problems, you can improve customer loyalty and increase your company's profits. Companies rely on such feedback, since this is the only way that they get to know if they are doing well in the market and what can be done to increase customer loyalty.

While analyzing your enhanced customer advantage, the areas you need to include are:

- Analyzing your customers core needs
- Interpreting customer satisfaction into loyalty
- Identifying strategies to transform a difficult customer into a loyal customer
- Estimating the value of your customers

Some questions that you need to consider while you estimate customer satisfaction:

- How can you measure your customer satisfaction? What is the prevailing trend to measure this factor?
- How do you know that your measurement is accurate and relevant?

- Who is your target audience and what are their basic needs?
- What do you consider to be a profitable customer? What attracts them towards your business?
- What are you doing to gain customer loyalty?
- How are your customers segregated?
- What kind of data do you collect that analyzes this customer segregation?
- How can you compare this segregation and their performance with the previous three years?

Putting down the core advantages of your company based on the above categories is the best way to realize the potential growth of your business. In fact, a lot of businesses troubleshoot problems in difficult areas when they sit down to put together a competitive business analysis.

The reason why most businesses need to reassure themselves that their business is working on almost every segment of their organization is to maintain a healthy workforce and develop new strategies to enhance profit. Until and unless a business is sure about the advantage it has over its competitors, it will never know how to succeed and out-perform their competition. A critical analysis of the functioning of the company and the advantages it has over its competitors can also be a contributing factor to most marketing strategies.

This wraps up the makings of an Irresistible Business Plan, but before we go on to Grant Writing Made Easy, if you have more questions on business plans, there's great information at SBA.gov.

SAMPLE BUSINESS PLAN

EXECUTIVE SUMMARY

COWBIZ CENTRAL Clothing is a brand-new western apparel store that caters to the African-American community in Texas. As the name says it, we focus on producing western apparel and accessories and wish to position ourselves at the top of this retail market.

Being the first African-American apparel store that caters to the cowboy community in Texas, we aim to achieve 80% of the market share and become one of the most trusted shopping hub for local population as well as those who enjoy wearing western wear globally.

COWBIZ CENTRAL Clothing is located at 608.5 N. Harwood, Dallas, TX 75201 USA. Being a state-of-the-art apparel store, COWBIZ CENTRAL has centralized itself among the African-American residential location and intend to actively involve in social activities of our target market. We believe that this proactive integration is important for our initial success and for our long-term growth potential.

Objectives

- We wish to create a shopping scenario that specially serves the apparel needs of urban and modern African-American community.
- Be aimed at targeting 75% of the market share and become the top-rated ethnic western wear clothing store in the whole of Texas and achieve a trusted name in the local cowboy community.
- We target a margin of 50% profit in the first year itself
- We are aiming to have a customer base of around

house and by the end of the initial year.

- We are targeting a net profit of $90,000 by the second year and $210,000 by the 3th year.
- We wish to actively involve and become the voice of the local community and support advocates are events and encourage education among children.

Mission

COWBIZ CENTRAL Western Wear's mission is to offer the finest quality in western wear that can be closely associated with the culture of the cowboy community.

Key to Success

In order to be the most successful brand in western wear apparels, COWBIZ CENTRAL needs to follow:

- A collection of sizes that can affect effect almost every body structure of the African-American target audience.
- Provide the finest customized service in an ambience of Southern hospitality.
- Focus on marketing and advertising the brand among the target audience to help them know more about the brand and its retail locations.
- Do constant review of our stock and sales, so that we can maintain a sustainable inventory level.

COMPANY DESCRIPTION

COWBIZ CENTRAL Clothing is formed on a partnership basis with Vance Scott and Christopher Chapman being the two partners.

As stated the store will be located at 608.5 N. Harwood, Dallas, TX 75201 USA, as it is regarded to be the shopping hub among the African-American community in the north central side of Texas.

The operational hours of the retail store would be Monday–Thursday (10 AM to 6 PM), Tuesday –Friday (10 AM to 9 PM) and Saturday –Sunday (1 PM to 8 PM). The times are subject to change according to any promotional activities or special festive/shopping season.

All the inventory and merchandise will be produced and purchased according to the company's value and mission. On merchandise we focus on producing various sizes including plus sizes for men and women.

Company ownership

COWBIZ CENTRAL Clothing is formed on a partnership basis with Vance Scott and Christopher Chapman being the two partners, who will be in charge of all the managerial and administrative duties of the company.

MARKET ANALYSIS

The main target audience of COWBIZ CENTRAL Clothing is the African-American community located in the north central part of Texas. Since we are located in the central part of the residential community, we have already penetrated into a large percentage of our customer base.

Our second target audience would be the Hispanic community that continues to grow at a steady rate along the South central area. We aim to slowly penetrate into this community as well as they follow western clothing closely.

The third target audience of COWBIZ CENTRAL has been listed as other. As the popularity of the store as well as the brand increases we expect to serve various curious shoppers and local residents who wish to purchase during the discount season.

Segmentation of the target audience

Most of the African-American cowboy community is concentrated along the southwestern part of the city, which will be our highest concentration of target audience.

The Hispanic community is steady growing in number along the areas where the retail store is located. This community has been showing steady interest and has high potential of becoming a loyal customer of western wear. Right now we have studied their interest in famous Western brands like Wrangler.

Since COWBIZ CENTRAL as a variety of southwestern and western clothing along with numerous accessories and gifts, we feel that our potential customers that are labeled as 'others' will attract many curious shoppers. Our exotic ambience and excellent customer service will force them to come back again to the store.

Market Growth

The market growth has been studied to go towards an upward motion even though some of the latest economic downturns have affected the north central part of Texas. Although, for the time being, this part of Texas is facing an economic change by the end of the second half of next year, Texas with see high positive growth in the employment and shopping front.

Dallas has been projected to be one of the best cities in the entire United States to start a new business and has been ranked as the best place for new business growth. The latest survey shows that 25,000 new local businesses were started in Dallas.

Competitors:

COWBIZ CENTRAL Clothing has 3 competitors within 20 miles radius of its retail store location.

Seplers Boot Store - located approximately 8 miles from our location is the closest competitor. The brand is known to be the largest in western wear in the entire Texas area. They operate 40 retail stores and sell basic western wear and boots. They are preferred by most people because of the size of their store, which have bought them a big percentage of the market share. However, finding plus sizes for men and women in the store would be extremely difficult and they are a step back in offering current western wear styles.

Costa Frame - located approximately 10 miles from our store. The place has been combined with a barbecue restaurant with shopping in the prime tourist attraction. They offer a wide range of western apparel, gift items, food products and grills. They are not much into advertising or promotions, so if you do not visit their store personally you would never know about their establishment.

Black Stallion - this is located approximately 20 miles from our store and is the furthest of all our competitors. This is a family owned business and has to stores in the whole Texas. Their customer base seems to be more improvised since they carry contemporary western style apparels. They also offer bedding and housewares along with a few plus sizes for men and women. Black Stallion lags in advertising and promotional front.

MANAGEMENT AND ORGANIZATION

COWBIZ CENTRAL being a very small business requires a very simple organizational structure where the partners that act as general managers. They will be responsible for all the administrative, purchasing, marketing and inventory control. We are looking forward to hire 2 sales representatives and one store manager.

PRODUCTS AND SERVICES

COWBIZ CENTRAL Clothing will cater nationally recognized African-American western wear. Our selection would range from the trendy style of Western ethics to the basics of Wrangler. We will be purchasing our merchandise through manufacturers and sales representatives in numerous colors, sizes and styles to fit our target audience. The largest amount of merchandise will be in apparel followed by western accessories, shoes and gifts.

The organization would rely on customer suggestions, feedback, survey, sales report to remove or introduce any new operational needs.

MARKETING STRATEGY

COWBIZ CENTRAL Clothing aims to use our target audience advertising and sales promotion to generate publicity and create a loyal customer base. For this we intend to produce:

- 3000 full color flyer with 20% coupon on shopping. This would be freely distributed throughout the southern part of Texas, African-American communities, cowboy dance parties, gatherings, rodeos and other associated venues, two weeks prior to the opening of the store.
- We will be issuing 300 grand invitations and mailing them to potential customers two weeks in advance to the opening of the store. The invitation but also include

a 20% discount coupon for the first purchase. This customer base will be sourced from word-of-mouth community involvement.

- We would also be issuing 3000 business cards with COWBIZ CENTRAL Clothing Shopping Card on the reverse side, which will allow a customer to get 20% discount after every 10 purchases.
- We will also conduct a social media promotion through our Facebook page, which has over 5,000 fans as well as our Instagram and Twitter pages, which have 12,000 followers combined.

FUNDING

COWBIZ CENTRAL Clothing incorporation cost is listed in the appendix. The company will be initiated within three months after the inventory has been made available in their respective destination. The major part of the company's asset will exist in the merchandising. The cash on balance on the opening day will be $400.

The main aim of this business plan is to secure a funding of $17,700 Accion loan. This additional financing is required to work on the inventory, retail premises and any other operational costs. The loan will be projected as the company's long-term liability along with other financing needs. Additional financing they include the partners to invest $6000 and a short-term expense of $3000 for inventory replacement whenever needed.

Effective administration and creating a loyal customer base will allow COWBIZ CENTRAL Clothing to be independent of all financial obligations and bring profits in the second year of its start up.

CORE BUSINESS ADVANTAGE

COWBIZ CENTRAL Clothing has a distinctive advantage that would make us the number one brand in our niche, out beat any competition and build a loyal customer base.

- We are the only and the first African-American family operated western wear retail store in Texas.
- We will be introducing 'COWBIZ CENTRAL Shopping discount card' which will entitle our customers to a 20% discount after every 10 purchases.
- We have plus sized clothing, which would fit almost any body structure.
- We will be actively involving into the culture and bonding of the African-American community. This would make our target audience relate more to our products.
- Our location has been centered among the target audience.
- We will be having an extensive report of each customer, their residential address, the number of purchases, the size they prefer and their shopping trends. This would help us to follow up with our customer and contact them in case of any in-house promotional offers.

GRANT WRITING MADE EASY

AN OVERVIEW

As a non-profit organization or individual, in order to fund your projects and ideas there will be a need to write and submit a grant proposal to secure funding. A grant proposal is basically a compelling presentation as to why a funder should give you money. Grant proposals are important for the both the funder and the organization requesting money. It allows the funder an opportunity to learn more about your organization and your current and future projects. For the organization submitting the grant, this is an excellent opportunity to outline your project ideas and present a comprehensive explanation of your organization. Grant proposals provide organizations a means to discuss the services and programs provided currently and how future funding will allow your organization to expand in order to provide additional opportunities.

When presenting a grant to a funder, especially a new funder, it's very important to be concise yet thorough in your application. This is your one opportunity to explain several things including your qualifications, accomplishments, results, plan for evaluation and most of all how this will not only benefit the community but the funder, as well.

After you have selected a funder that fits your organization and reviewed their funding options, request the grant instructions and application from the funder. Most grant proposals have several components that must be completed. When applying for a grant always allow enough time to complete the application thoroughly and correctly. Read through the entire instructions and application, making note of key things including the deadline, page limit, contacts and guidelines. After you have reviewed the grant application, the next step is writing the grant.

Most grant instructions give specific outlines that must be followed for submission. This is your opportunity to detail your organization, your project, staff, program, method of evaluation, why you are requesting funding and the budget. When writing a grant proposal use an active voice and avoid jargon and technical words. The proposal should be easy to read and understand. It is also important to have more than one person review the final document when possible and assist with editing the final document. Make certain the document is formatted in a simple manner using fonts and sizing that is easy to read. It is also important to spell check and make certain that the budget is correct.

Grant applications typically have the following components: Cover Letter, Executive Summary, Statement of Need, Project Description, Budget, Organization Information and Conclusion. Most funders will allow organizations to send supplemental materials like DVDs, CDs, posters and other materials. Always check before submitting anything not specifically requested, and any materials submitted should have a direct connection to the program and organization. Sending a brochure or a PSA is a way to provide the funder a personal connection to the organization, but sending a DVD of some event that has no clear connection to your organization could actually have the opposite affect intended.

The final grant proposal that your organization submits will tell the funder a great deal about your organization. If it follows the instructions and guidelines, is well-written and easy to read, clear and concise and most of all complete, this lets the funder know that you are worthy of funding because you know how to follow instructions. This indicates to the funder that you are capable of performing the tasks of the program thus putting your organization in a good light. Many proposals are rejected simply because the package is incomplete and the organization didn't do as instructed.

Many organizations seek funding from multiple organizations and agencies, so it's always best to develop a basic grant proposal and budget. This general proposal will explain your project to a general audience. Before you submit proposals to different grant programs, it will need to be changed and edited to fit the organizations' specific funding guidelines and priorities.

Although each funding agency will have its own (usually very specific) requirements, there are several elements of a proposal that are fairly standard, and they often come in the following order:

Cover Letter- This is a brief letter of introduction to your organization and provides the requested amount. It should be on the organization's stationary.

Executive Summary- This is the most important portion of the proposal. It provides the overall statement of your request and the summary of the entire proposal. It encapsulates all of the key information and should be compelling in order to convince the funder that the project should be considered for support. It is important to include the problem or need the organization is prepared to address. This should include a brief description of the project including what will occur, as well as who and how many people will benefit from the project, how and where it will take place, the length of time of operation and the staff needed to perform the duties of the program. It is also important to include funding requirements including an explanation of the amount required to fund the program as well as future plans for funding the project. Also include a brief history of the organization and its expertise in the field. Include the purpose of the organization, the activities and why the organization is qualified to helm the project. Often it is helpful to write the Executive Summary after the rest of the proposal has been written.

Statement of Need- This section instructs the funder as to why your project is crucial. This should include a statement of the problem with statistics, facts and evidence that support the need for the project. The Statement of Need should establish that your organization understands the problems, providing the background for the project and the need and relevance of the organization. Be sure to show how your project is different from other organizations and its uniqueness. This section needs to be persuasive yet succinct. It's important to find the right balance when presenting the needs statement. Don't overstate the problem or be overly emotional.

ProjectDescription-Thissectionshouldhavefivesubsections: objectives, methods, staffing/administration, evaluation and sustainability. Objectives are the measurable outcomes of the program and should be tangible, specific, concrete and achievable. Goals are conceptual and more abstract. The methods describe the specific activities that will take place to achieve the objectives. The methods allow the reader to visualize the implementation of the project and should be able to convince the funder your agency is capable of achieving the goals of the project. **Dis**cuss how your organization will collaborate with other organizations to achieve your goals. In today's world where funding is tight and more organizations are vying for the same funding pool, funders want to get more value from their donations. Explain staffing requirements in detail and make sure that staffing makes sense. Be very explicit about the skill sets of the personnel already in place and explain the necessary skill sets and functions of personnel you will recruit. The evaluation plan explains how you will ascertain whether your program has achieved its objectives or failed. There are several types of evaluation tools that can be utilized. One measures the product and the other analyzes the process and/or strategies. It's necessary to describe the manner in which evaluation of information will be collected and analyzed. Most evaluation plans use qualitative and quantitative data. Sustainability explains how you will continue the program when the funding cycle has ended. Be sure to explain if and how you plan to continue the program or if it is just a one-time project. Evidence of fiscal sustainability is very attractive to funders.

Organization (Experience or Capability) - This is the opportunity to tell your funder about your organization. Explain when your organization was established, its mission, how the proposal fits the organization's mission, describe the organization's structure, programs, leadership and special expertise. This should be written in two-pages or less. Describe your activities, the assistance provided, your audience and clients, any special or unusual needs they face and why they rely on your agency. Also be sure to note the number of people that rely on your organization.

Conclusion - This should be a paragraph or two and should state any future plans or follow up activities. It is also an opportunity to make a final appeal for your project. You can briefly reiterate what your organization wants to do and why it's important. Also stress why your organization needs the funding for the program.

Budget- The budget spells out project costs and usually consists of a spreadsheet or table with the budget detailed as line items and a budget narrative (also known as a budget justification) that explains the various expenses. Even when proposal guidelines do not specifically mention a narrative, be sure to include a one or two page explanation of the budget. Consider including an exhaustive budget for your project, even if it exceeds the normal grant size of a particular funding organization. Simply make it clear that you are seeking additional funding from other sources. This technique will make it easier for you to combine awards down the road should you have the good fortune of receiving multiple grants. Make sure that all budget items meet the funding agency's requirements. If a line item falls outside an agency's requirements (e.g. some organizations will not cover equipment purchases or other capital expenses), explain in the budget justification that other grant sources will pay for the item.

Letters of Support - If the funder allows supplemental materials to be included; letters of support can boost your profile with the funder. Letters of support can come from several resources. They can be written by current clients discussing the positive impact your organization has had on their lives, other agencies you will be working with on the proposed project, consultants of the proposed project and community leaders. Letters of support should indicate enthusiasm for the proposed project and be positive. They should detail their experience with your organization and any proposed work they plan to do with the project and organization.

Letter of Inquiry - Many funders will request an initial letter proposal before requesting a full grant proposal. This is also called a Letter of Inquiry. A letter proposal should follow the same format of a full proposal but with less detail and more brevity. It should be no more than three pages. While it might be difficult to state all the information needed in this format it's very important to still include all of the necessary information in a more concise manner. The components of a letter proposal should follow the guidelines:

1. State the reason for writing and the amount requested.

2. Explain the need for the project or program.

3. Describe what your organization will do with the funds and the impact of the program upon its completion.

4. Provide organizational information including the mission statement, description of current programs offered, number of people served and staff, volunteer and board data.

5. Include budget information for the program as well as future funding opportunities.

6. Close the letter with a strong concluding statement and even offer to provide additional information to the funder.

7. Attachments can be included such as a board list, IRS determination letter, financial documentation and staff resumes.

Even though a letter proposal seems brief and simple, it's actually just as difficult to write as a full grant proposal. It is just as much of a challenge to decide what to include and how to write this information in a compelling and interesting manner. Many times this is the first glimpse the funder has into your organization. It's imperative to make every contact you have with the funder a positive stepping-stone to a future and lasting relationship.

Strong grant proposals take a long time to develop. Start the process early and leave time to get feedback from several readers on different drafts. Many times funders will supply a criterion for rating and evaluating proposals so be certain to follow their guidelines.

Types of Grants

When writing grant proposals it's very important to understand the different types of grants available to non-profit organizations requesting funding. There are several different types of grants awarded by foundations, corporations and government agencies. They each address a specific funding need. The grants include the following:

-Capacity Building Grants support initiatives that allow non-profits to operate. Capacity building typically refers to developing business skills that sustain the organization, developing the capability to communicate more effectively with supporters and donors and developing the capability to raise needed funds. Examples can include training for board members, management training for staff members, website, newsletter and brochure development, fees for consultants for fundraisers and strategic planning

-Capital Grants support the purchase, construction and expansion of real property or the purchase of equipment. These grants can be used to purchase a building, a computer or a van. When making a request for a capital grant, it's important to focus on how this purchase will help your organization to serve its clients better. It's also important to focus on the organization's future financial stability and health, so that the organization supplying funding will feel secure in making such a large donation to the organization.

-Challenge or Matching grants are awarded when conditions set by the foundation are met. This typically means the funder will award a certain amount when the nonprofit has raised the same amount from other resources. The grant will not be awarded unless the organization has successfully raised the agreed upon amount.

-Endowment grants are made to augment a non-profit's investment fund. Some non-profits will set aside a certain amount of funds to be invested and only spends the interest. Originally only large non-profits such as hospitals or universities had endowments, but more and more smaller non-profits are starting endowments.

-General Support or Operating grants are used to support the non-profit's day-to-day operations. These funds can be used to support anything from paying utilities to supporting program expenses. These funds can also be used to pay other administrative costs. While most funders prefer to pay for specific programs and services, some are aware that non-profits need to pay salaries and other expenses.

-Project or Program Grants are restricted funds to be used to fund specific programs. The funds can only be used for a connected set of activities with a beginning and end and specific costs.

-Seed grants are used to start a new program or a new non-profit organization. The funds are used to help smaller and startup organizations get their organizations and programs up and running. Seed grants can be used to pay for salaries or the actual costs of a program. The idea is to give an organization a strong push forward so that it can devote the majority of its time and energy to the organization and programs without having to worry about funding. Most seed grants are multi-year and decrease with each subsequent year of award.

-Unrestricted grants allow non-profits to use the funds awarded where they are most needed. There are no rules or guidelines to follow when utilizing these funds. The organization can choose how best to spend these funds.

Types of Foundations

There are many organizations that provide funding to non-profits. They include government, including state, city and local, corporations, and foundations, both private and public. A foundation is a nonprofit organization that supports charitable activities in order to serve the common good. A private foundation's funds come from one source, whether an individual, a family, or a corporation. A public foundation, in contrast, normally receives its assets from multiple sources, which may include private foundations, individuals, government agencies, and fees for service. Moreover, a public foundation must continue to seek money from diverse sources in order to retain its public status.

Some foundations have broad discretion regarding the charitable causes to which their grants can be directed. Others are very limited, often legally, by the order of the foundation donor. Some foundations are restricted to making grants only to specific causes while others must restrict their grant making to a specific geographic area.

Foundations are typically governed by stricter regulations than public charities, which generally raise money from the public to operate institutions or programs. Both foundations and public charities might use the term "foundation" in their titles, but very different laws apply to each.

There are several kinds of foundations and funders. Each has a specific organizational structure and operates in a different manner with respect to grant seekers. Many have geographical limitations, as well.

Private Foundations are the most common types of foundations. They are generally endowed, usually from a single individual or family. Private foundations frequently are also considered family foundations if relatives of the original donor are still active on the board of trustees or in the operation of the foundation. Independent Foundations have no relative of the donor involved in the grant making process. A private foundation's grant decisions may be made by the original donor, by members of the donor's family, by an appointed board of directors or by a bank trust officer acting on the donor's behalf. Trustee decision or the will of the donor often limits the geographic and interest areas of these foundations.

Corporate Foundations are also private foundations. They are independent grant making organizations whose originating donor is a corporation rather than a family or individual. They may have an actual endowment, or they may receive annual funding from the corporation. Grant making decisions are usually made by a board of directors consisting of top corporate management, local corporate officers, employee committees and sometimes outside community members.

Some companies operate in-house corporate giving programs, which unlike corporate foundations are under the full control of the company and are not required by law to follow the same regulations. Many corporations maintain both a foundation and a corporate giving program. Geographical range is often limited to areas where there is a corporate presence and active employee presence.

Corporate Giving Programs are functionally similar to corporate foundations, except that they are not legally foundations and therefore are not required by law to grant a certain percentage of assets or to publicly disclose their grant making activities. Many corporations run both a foundation and a giving program, coordinating the grant making activities of the two groups. Often the giving program works closely with their company's marketing and public relations departments as well as the employees. Their grant making tends to focus on the educational, cultural and social welfare needs of the communities where the donor corporation's facilities and employees are located. Hey will also focus on educational areas that will produce future employees. They typically exist to enhance the corporate image.

Public Foundations are publicly supported charitable organizations that receive much of their financial support in the form of contributions from the general public. There are many types of public foundations including community foundations. Public foundations support a variety of interest areas with or without geographic limitations as defined in their organizing charter and/or by their governing boards. The public foundations primarily make grants to multiple beneficiaries and derive the majority of their funding revenues from a single source, usually an endowment built from charitable gifts.

Community Foundations are public foundations made up of a considerable number of individual endowments managed by a single administrative body with all the funds pooled for greater investment return. As their name implies, community foundations usually have a very distinct and limited geographical area. Some of the individual funds are general purpose and discretionary; others are quite narrowly focused and may offer funds only for scholarships or a certain group of organizations. The trustees are chosen from the public for a specific term. The board typically has full discretionary responsibility over some funds while some funds may be donor-advised and others directed to a particular agency or organization.

Special Interest and Operating Foundations restrict their grants to a special field of interest or community type. They are very specialized with a very narrow focus and scope. There are many types of special interest philanthropic entities, such as federated funds (United Way), giving circles (these can be formal or informal), pooled funds, and organizations that don't fit into any of these other categories but still make donations.

Writing a successful grant proposal takes advance planning and preparation, whether you are a new grant writer or a seasoned professional. It takes coordination, research, advance planning and preparation to write and package your proposal to prepare for submission and follow-up.

It is imperative when organizing your proposal to pay attention to the details and specifications of the instructions of the funder. When writing use concise, persuasive writing, and request reasonable funding. Before you begin to write, review the grant in its entirety making certain you understand the grant maker's guidelines. Always make sure the grant maker's goals and objectives match your grant seeking purposes.

When applying for a grant, it's very important to know what type of funding requests they accept. Grants are given for a variety of reasons, which can include specific programs, general operating and unrestricted grants.

Preparation is vital to the grant-writing process. It is important to have solid planning and research to simplify the writing stage.

When writing the components of the grant make sure that you can clearly deliver an answer to the need you have detailed or a solution to the problem you have described, based on your organization's experience and ability. It's important to describe why the funding is critical to the success of your program.

While researching prospective funders and grant makers, make certain you are actually eligible to submit a proposal to them. When writing your proposal, make certain they're appropriate for your organization. Always research several potential funding sources and don't limit your funding options to just one potential funder. Once you have found potential funders, make contact with them to make certain you have a clear understanding of their guidelines and requirements

When writing a grant proposal follow these helpful guidelines

1. Always state your organization's needs and objectives clearly and concisely. While preparing your grant choose your words wisely and be economical in word choices. It's very important to use active voice, correct grammar not jargon and proper spelling. Your grant should be factual and clear but most of all professional.
2. Always state clearly in the grant why you are seeking the grant, your plans for funding and why you are the

perfect match for the funder. Your grant should follow the funder's guidelines but it should also stand out in a sea of other submissions. It's important to make your grant unique, interesting and most of all persuasive.

3. When writing your grant think ahead to the next funding cycle. If your grant is declined, speak to someone at the organizaiton to get feedback as to why your grant was rejected. This will allow opportunity to revise any unsuccessful proposals and prepare to resubmit it during the next funding cycle. By establishing a relationship with funders you are opening opportunites for more grants and funding in the future. Always submit progress reports and final final reports on time and in a professional manner.

Following the submission of the final grant proposal always keep in mind that funders typically turn down many more proposals than they fund. If your proposal should be denied, don't fret. Sometimes funders choose to focus their grant making on specific programs and services and your proposal fell outside of their parameters. Many times when funders send letters of denial they will provide specific reasons for the decision.

If you are lucky enough to receive funding, it's very important to perform as promised. Many times you or an officer of your organization must complete a grant agreement confirming tax-exempt status. Many request periodic updates as well as a final report at the end of the funding cycle. It's important to be prepared to offer proof of evaluation and program status. Always stay in contact with the funder and send them any publicity, newsletters, memos and letters that state the progress and success of your program. Most funders will require that their support be mentioned in any press release or literature about the specific program they have funded. While its always important to always be on the look out for other funding resources, its also important to keep good relationships with current funders. Some organizations believe that always going to the same organizations for funding might deplete resources for their agency. If you have always done great job and utlized funding responsibly, this establishes you as a good potential grant recipient. Current funders will help you as much as possbile even if they're not able to continue funding your project. This will allow them to refer you to other funders that can provide funding.

4. When writing the grant it's very important to follow the instructions carefully. Always provide all the information asked for in the application instructions in the order requested. Prior to writing the grant, make a list of everything you are going to need and the questions you need to answer in order to write the grant. Make note of everything that you might need to write the grant including data, statistics, support documents, staff resumes and experience, forms and signatures. Be sure to submit the grant proposal by the time and date specified. Any late proposals will not be considered, even if they are a few minutes past the deadline.

5. It's very important to communicate in a clear and concise manner and always justify everything especially budget items. Be very clear and state accurately what you will do, how you will do it and why it is important. When structuring the document use headings and format for readability. When designing the document, left-justify and leave a reasonable amount of white space in the document. Pay attention to any instructions for formatting requirements, as well.

General Tips

1. Begin early.
2. Apply early and often.
3. Don't forget to include a cover letter with your application.
4. Answer all questions.
5. If rejected, revise your proposal and apply again.
6. Give them what they want. Follow the application guidelines exactly.
7. Be explicit and specific.
8. Be realistic in designing the project.
9. Make explicit the goals and objectives of your program plan for evaluation of the results and future plans for the program.
10. Follow the application guidelines exactly. (We have repeated this tip because it is very, very important.)

Whether your proposal receives funding will rely in large part on whether your purpose and goals closely match the priorities of granting agencies. Locating possible grantors is a time consuming task, but in the long run it will yield the greatest benefits. Even if you have the most appealing grant proposal in the world, if you don't send it to the right agency, then you're unlikely to receive funding.

There are many sources of information about granting agencies and grant programs. There are many online resources available including The Foundation Center and the Corporate Giving Directory as well as many at most public libraries. There are also many location-based directories and program interest-based directories. Be careful of any online organization offering a database that requires payment for access to funding resources. With careful and diligent research finding funding sources that match your needs can be obtained. Most cities have organizations that assist non-profits with these needs as well. They will direct you to online databases, books and journals that will be very helpful to you in your research. Also look to organizations that are larger than your own and offering similar services and research their funders.

Organization is key when writing grant proposals and contacting potential funders. Included are several forms that will allow you to track any contact with potential funders and your progress with grant applications. When researching potential funders, it's important to remember key elements including when initial contact has been made and any follow-up necessary for future funding possibilities. If there are several people working on a grant application, a check-list form will allow you to assign responsibilities, due dates and progress. When writing a grant organization is key to a timely submission.

In conclusion, preparation is vital to the grant-writing process. Solid planning and research will simplify the writing stage. A well-written proposal follows the basic steps outlined below.

1. Research grant makers, including funding purposes and applicant eligibility.

2. Determine whether the grant makers' goals and objectives match your grant seeking purposes.

3. Target your proposal to grant makers appropriate to your field and project and never limit your funding request to just one source.

4. Contact the grant maker; before you write your proposal, to be sure you clearly understand the grant maker's guidelines and requirements.

5. Prove that you have a significant need or problem in your proposal.

6. Deliver an answer to the need, or solution to the problem. Make sure your proposal describes a program/project for change.

7. Reflect solid and good planning, research and vision throughout your proposal.

8. Present your proposal in the appropriate and complete format, and include all required attachments.

9. State your organization's needs and objectives clearly and concisely. Write well. Do not waste words. Use active rather than passive verbs. Use proper grammar and correct spelling. Be clear, factual, supportable, and professional. A well-written proposal is a key factor in the grant maker's decision-making process.

10. Be clear about why you are seeking a grant, how the money will be utilized, and you fit with the grant maker's priorities. Prepare an interesting, persuasive and unique proposal.

11. Cover the following criteria: project purpose, community need, funds needed, and skills and competence.

12. The application should provide an answer for the following: Who are you? How do you qualify? What do you want? What problem will you address and how? Who will benefit and how? What specific objectives will you accomplish and how? How will you measure your results? How does your funding request comply with the grant maker's purpose, goals and objectives?

13. Demonstrate your method of evaluation and be sure to include any community support. Specify the project's goals and measurable objectives and quantified outcomes.

14. Always follow the exact specifications of the grant makers in their applications, Requests for Proposals (RFPs) and guidelines.

15. Follow-up with the grant maker about the status, evaluation, and outcome of your proposal, after it is submitted. Request feedback about your proposal's strengths and weaknesses.

SAMPLE GRANT

Name: ORGANIZATION NAME

Mailing Address:

Physical Address:

Phone Number:

Fax Number:

Contact Person:

Email Address:

Website:

Mission Statement: The mission of our organization is to provide services to youth with incarcerated parents to assist them in maintaining the family bond.

Organizational Summary:

Please accept this request from our organization to be considered for funding from your organization in the amount of $5,000. Our primary focus is to empower youth whose parents are incarcerated by providing a support system in a caring, inclusive, and learning environment. Through our program, we are committed to inspiring youth to succeed by instilling a sense of hope for the future and strengthening the parental relationship by lessening the impact of separation due to incarceration.

Our organization was founded in 2011 by John Doe. Due to his own experience with having incarcerated parents, he had first-hand knowledge of the importance of community programs to assist youth. Many youth with incarcerated parents are in need of community support to break the cycle. He believes with a structured program instilling self-esteem to youth will help create a positive impact on these at-risk youth to make better choices so that they can live better lives.

The organization will provide assistance and social services to those in the greatest of need in Los Angeles, CA communities.

Statement of Need:

Children are the foundation of the future of our community and their success is directly paired to the success of our communities and society. On any given day, over 1.5 million children in this country have a parent who is incarcerated, with a significant number of children in the Los Angeles area alone. Related to this is the increasing number of parents who are incarcerated, which has nearly doubled in the past 20 years. The U.S. Bureau of Justice Statistics reports nearly 60,000 youth are in state and federal prisons in California. We offer various programs designed to empower and enrich the lives of youth with an incarcerated parent. Knowing that the cycle, which often accompanies incarceration, can be broken, we provide an environment that provides enrichment, self-esteem and a positive life-enhancing program that encourages the youth to succeed by using life's stumbling blocks as stepping-stones.

Helping those most in need places a strain on government resources that already can barely provide the very basic needs of those already most severely financially and socially impacted and suffering. Our state resources are already quite limited and funding for programs to provide for children and adolescents with needs such as mental health issues, substance abuse, family violence and education are unfortunately already over extended and fragmented.

According to the Juvenile Section of the Los Angeles Community Plan 2013, whether a family is two parent, single parent, extended family or non relative, they all face the same daily challenges of survival and have the same desires for a good life for their children. Some families face more challenges than others and those families need the help and support that a community that cares can only provide. Issues such as joblessness, lack of education, linguistic difference, child development, substance abuse, mental health and/or family violence are multi-generational leaving most families with too few resources to help guide youth that are already in greatest of need to raise children that have the potential for a positive future. Many families lack emotional, financial or social stability that youth need when growing and learning to be well balanced.

We will provide expanded and extended support to those youth most in need of services and support. We are acutely aware of the needs of these youth in crisis and can help make the transition to build better lives and make it possible for them to be productive members of society. Youth that live in female-headed single parent homes are more likely to live in poverty and more likely to score lower on measurements of health, education and emotional and behavioral problems than children living with both parents. These children are also more likely to drop out of school, earn less money and as adults become single parents themselves. One of the main objectives with the programs of the organization is the break this cycle and teach youth to be self-sufficient and teach them that there are options in society that allow them obtain goals that had previously been unobtainable, to become productive members of society and live productive and successful lives.

Youth in Los Angeles County need assistance in their transition from children to young adults more than ever today given the economic struggles faced in today's society. Community programs that teach youth how to break the cycle of incarceration are in great need and are of huge importance. Programs that teach adolescents and soon-to-be adults adequate life skills and training and independent life support have a lesser chance of being part of the adult justice system. The programs we provide fit the models of support needed outlined by the County of Los Angeles to serve youth at risk are currently perfectly suited. The programs we provide are focused on prevention services and efforts that lead to lack of engagement with the Juvenile Justice System and adult justice system. The programs also provide extended prevention services that deter youth from delinquent behaviors, encourage school participation and involvement in activities and assist youth dealing with difficult at-home situations.

We are writing to ask that you consider selecting our organization as one of your foundation's grantees. As a recipient of your generous funding, we will be able to provide much needed support programs to the children of incarcerated parents who are in very desperate need for programs and services that are unique to their problems and issues. Our hope is to provide these youth, many of whom who are in much greater need than most due to their specific issues and problems, to become productive members of society regardless of their own troubled background. They have a greater need for help due to the incarceration of their parents and their extended family support is typically quite minimal.

We need your assistance now more than ever before because of the lack of services and programs that meet their needs and because their needs are typically lowest on the list of those that receive support services. It is only with your help and support that we can be of service and aid to these youth so that they can break the cycle of incarceration, drug abuse, early parenthood and become self-supporting youth with high self-esteem and high self-worth.

Program and Purpose of Funding

At our organization, the program that your funding will assist in supporting will provide services to youth with parents who are currently or who have been previously incarcerated: The Positive Future. Our program is distinct and designed with the needs of our participants past, present and future in mind.

The participants of the program will be recruited from a number of organizations that includes community programs; community services organizations, churches, jails, prisons, halfway houses, and other organizations that provide services to incarcerated youth and programs for youth. In order to measure the success of our program we will utilize qualitative and quantitative methods. We will request permission initially from the youth wanting to be members in the program and then from the incarcerated parent of each child. For participation purposes, this will allow for each youth's full cooperation in the program's activities and objectives.

Following their agreement to participate in the program, we will then provide each youth with an application to be completed. Part of the application process includes an individualized screening section, which will detail background, current situation including living and education, and future life plans and potential goals. Following acceptance to the program, they will each be given an individualized educational plan that is in part comprised of their goals, needs and wants expressed in the initial application process and evaluation plan.

We have given considerable consideration to our application and evaluation process prior to it being administered to our youth that is comprised of questions that will help us assist in achieving their optimal life plan. Our organization's series, activities and programs has been developed and will be provided by educated and expert facilitators and professionals that have extensive experience in psychology, prison and jail system and at risk youth, specifically. We're very serious about our responsibility to our youth. We feel each is an individual but also part of a team that expects full participation, feedback and peer support.

We utilize a three-tiered qualitative evaluation process that measures if the goals and objectives of our program have been achieved with each individual participant. The first evaluation is completed upon acceptance into the program to outline their personal and individual goals and objectives and plan activities and programs that will help them to achieve their personal plan. The second evaluation is performed during a midway period of their participation in the program to measure if their goals are being achieved at this period in the program and how best to assist them in their personal achievement process. The final evaluation will occur at the end of their participation in the program to fully measure if all of the goals and objectives outlined when they started the program had been achieved.

We have no specific timeline that states when a student has completed their participation in the program. We realize that each youth is unique and has a set of issues and problems that are specific to them and how they best complete their individual objectives. We're here to mentor each student and allow him or her to be individuals and treat them as such. There's no need for competition and we want to provide them with a vision that they can achieve in their own time and in their own way.

A portion of our evaluation process also includes receiving input from the youth to gather their personal evaluation of the program. We want to learn from our youth directly in regards to our successes, failures and needs of improvement our programs and activities and if they can better assist them with the outcomes we've designed and developed for them individually.

Positive Future

There are two goals to the components of the Positive Future Program that includes mentorship, community service, community involvement and life skills. With this program, the youth will develop real-world abilities that will last them throughout the course of their lifetime. Providing instruction in a manner that promotes individual success will provide the youth with guidance from professionals from a variety of fields who are committed to making a difference and will assist with the completion of the objectives. Our foundation is dedicated to assist our youth by providing them with the skills needed to become productive members of our society and encouraging them to give back what has been provided to them while members of our program.

The first goal ensures the cultivation of character development and generates positive self-worth. The program provides character cultivation workshops and resources that will enhance self-esteem, develop leadership and communication skills, demonstrate proper etiquette, establish cognizance of wellness, teach social and life skills and instill moral values. The workshops will also have several classes that focus on a variety of topics and skills that will empower each student and help them build better futures. The workshops will equip the youth with appropriate tools to become confident, positive-thinking and productive members of society.

Social skills workshops will include responsibility and accountability, forming trusting relationships, understanding and expressing emotions, increasing attention and listening, working cooperatively, handling peer pressure, and dealing with bullying and victimization. Topics will also include issues that deal with wellness and health such as the prevention of violence, teen pregnancy, STDs and HIV/AIDS education and prevention, the balance of mind, body and spirit and encourage youth to embrace and live a lifestyle that focuses on health and nutrition. We will also teach our youth to deal with stress management, humor and play and the meaning and purpose of spirituality. Our youth will enroll and attend four workshops annually.

The program also provides the youth an opportunity to give back to the community through service, by providing 8 total hours annually of non-profit volunteer service. This will strengthen the youth's sense of civic engagement and awareness. The youth will have the opportunity to deliberate, plan, implement, and reflect on their community service, thereby sustaining high-quality service learning.

The second goal of the Positive Future Program is to inspire the youth to succeed with the assistance of speakers and an individualized education process. We have a three-tier plan to help execute the goals of this program. The initial goal is to create individualized educational plans and to provide incentives when each goal has been achieved by our youth. We will also have outside speakers share their journeys of success despite obstacles in life by using their stumbling blocks as stepping-stones. We will also equip our youth with the appropriate tools to break the cycle of intergenerational incarceration to become productive youth of society.

The individualized plan allows for goal setting and following through on commitments to show our youth the importance of responsibility and accountability. Examples of accountability include maintaining grades, increasing and maintaining attendance and increased involvement in school leadership programs. Our qualitative method of measuring success is based on the total number of youth enrolled in the program; we have at least 75% of our youth to succeed in their Individual Educational Plan. We also measure our success by having 75% of our youth to attend our Speaker's Series and which will then lead to assist in at least 80% of our youth avoid contact with the Juvenile Justice System.

By providing our youth with training and mentoring, they can then help other youth in situations that are similar to theirs in the community to help improve and develop youth that are stronger and have increased self-esteem. This will also have the added affect of developing communities that are filled with youth that have pride where they reside. Newer and stronger futures are what we want to rebuild in our communities and for generations to come, to live, work, and raise families. We want to assist youth with any training needed to become better educated, gain better skills to increase their employability and to raise their self-esteem and teach them to become empowered and self-sufficient. We're also dedicated to motivate and empower our youth to embrace their beauty inside and out to achieve a renewed spirit, confidence and professionalism in order to experience their own personal success and growth.

In 2014, we plan to implement the inaugural session of the Positive Futures Program. Initial funding for the program will be $30, 400. Program costs includes: facility rental, travel of the youth to locations for training and support services, meals, facilitator program fees and consultancy costs, supplies and equipment, volunteer training and administrative costs. This funding will allow for the workshops, resources, training and mentorships for approximately 20 to 25 youth. In 2015, we hope to increase our services to provide for 35 to 45 youth.

Organization Information

We are a very unique organization that is most suited to provide the services needed for youth with incarcerated parents. Many of our personnel and the founder of the organization have personal experience with parental incarceration. This makes them well suited to organize and implement the programs and services of the organization to the youth of the community. With the city of Los Angeles relying heavily on community-based organizations to supplement the services needed in the community to help at risk youth, our organization is very unique due to its program and service delivery and lack of programs currently in the community. Our programs assist youth in reaching their full potential as members of society and to be productive citizens. The goals identified by Los Angeles County to assist youth are already goals that are currently a significant portion of the goals that are primary to our programs.

We focus to provide youth with opportunities to learn new skills and engage in character building activities, to develop meaningful relationships with adult role models and peers and incentives to stay in school and become successful citizens. We also provide peer support to youth and to their parents post incarceration.

Our programs also invests in comprehensive development programs and out of school programs, provides youth with developing supportive relationships with their parents during and post incarceration, and provides them with an opportunity to have a sense of belonging to an organization to build self-esteem and feelings of self worth. The organization assists the youth with learning social norms while valuing their input in the organization to increase their sense of empowerment and participation. We also assist the youth with giving back to society. We try to promote partnerships with other organizations to build a team of services that promotes other youth to give back to the community at large.

The goals of the programs will support the reduction of anti-social attitudes and rebellious behavior, such as drug use and violence. The program also provides youth with educational assistance such as tutoring and mentorships. The program encourages youth to participate in school, attend classes, excel in their work, increase their grades, and most importantly, complete their education. The mentorships developed allows the youth the opportunity to have a long-term relationship that will provide the youth with educational opportunities that will lead them to college and/or university, alternative educational programs or other career assessment opportunities.

We also provide substantial efforts and opportunities to youth to break the generational cycle of incarceration through mentorship programs and social programs.

Plan for Evaluation of Program

Our method to evaluate our program will be both qualitative and quantitative. Prior to admittance and acceptance potential clients will be requested to complete an application.

Our team of program facilitators will administer a pre-test, mid-term test and post-test to our youth in order to measure what information is learned by the participants during the length of our program, At the conclusion of each session, we will also ask the facilitators to complete a detailed evaluation questionnaire so we can continue to find ways to improve our programs and develop innovative and new methods to keep our participants engaged and fulfilled by our programs.

We will also regularly evaluate our program using internal and external professionals and program evaluators. One of our goals is to teach our youth to become stellar members of society and reach the members fullest potential as members of the community. We're always working to develop sophisticated, yet practical evaluation processes in order to measure the long-term impact of our programs on the youth who participate in our organization. We're striving to have the best program in Los Angeles County which provides opportunities that can allow for replication of the organization to other communities across the nation that are facing the same need for similar or exact services to at-risk youth.

The project will collect data from our participants based on utilizing tools that measure their needs, evaluate if their needs had been achieved and collect information regarding the need for future projects and programs that should be implemented to further satisfy their needs.

Our evaluation will include the following components:

· Design and conduct an evaluation that utilizes both qualitative and quantitative methods to determine if our program is producing its intended effects.

· We will strategically plan activities that will achieve the program goals and objectives

· Respond to the information gathered during the evaluation process to improve, change or develop programs.

· Design and implement any new programs that will improve the future success of programs and if our goals and objectives were achieved.

· Utilize the data collected during the evaluation process to make adjustments in service delivery and improve the overall program

The success of our program will include:
- All youth take personal responsibility for implementation of goals.
- Youth engage in service to others.
- Youth are supported, educated, and equipped to become successful members of society.
- Youth are provided with opportunities to receive frequent expressions of support in both informal settings and during our programs.
- Youth are given opportunities to promote caring, clear boundaries and sustained relationships with adults.
- Youth have opportunities to serve, lead, and make decisions.

Other Similar Programs

While there are other community organizations that provide programs that are similar none offer the same services that are specifically for youth of incarcerated parents such as our organization. We're always looking for opportunities to partner with other organizations. We offer our programs to any organization that needs our services and request our assistance when there is a need for any of our programs and services identified.

Additional and Requested Funding Sources

In order to provide our services to the youth and parents of our programs we have requested funding from many sources to provide both operational and program services. Funding has been requested from the following organizations: Nordstrom Cares, Bank of America, Meadows Foundation, Walgreens Foundation, Rees-Jones Foundation and the Macy's Foundation.

Conclusion:

In conclusion, by funding our organization, your support will assist the goals of young people who will thrive in a society that otherwise consider supporting them to be of lesser importance and need. There is an unfortunate stigma that is placed on youth and children with an incarcerated parent. Many of these youth feel isolated and alone with no one to reach out to who will understand their unusual need for support and services. The leaders of this organization have an understanding of the importance of programs that teaches these youth that they are important and needed as members of society. We assist them in building lives that have a vision, purpose and importance that is achievable. We teach them to learn and harness their own power and become leaders. We realize its hard work that is needed to help these youth but we have the ability to assist them. We want them to have pride in themselves and to be independent.

It is only with your funding assistance we can provide these services and programs. Without it, many youth who are in great need will be forgotten by society and not reach their fullest potential. Your funding will assist thousands of at-risk youth's self-esteem and self-importance.

BUDGET

	COST	REQUESTED	BALANCE
1. Personal Items	$3,000.00	$1,500.00	$1,000.00
2. Support Group Funding	$3,000.00	$1,500.00	$1,000.00
3. Salaries for Program Staff	$7,000.00	$0.00	$7,000.00
4. Direct Service Needs Assistance	$2,500.00	$250.00	$1,000.00
5. Transportation	$1,500.00	$1,500.00	$300.00
6. Facility Rental	$1,400.00	$250.00	$750.00
Total	$18,400.00	$5,000.00	$10,700.00

GRANT TRACKING FORM

Name of funder: _____

Contact Person/Title: _____

Address:_____

City/State/Zip: _____

Phone:_____Fax: _____

Email_____Web site: _____

Other contact information: _____

_____

Past support received (if any): Amount: _____Date: _____

Purpose/Allocated for:_____

Funding cycle: _____

Date to submit request:_____

Process/Instructions: _____

_____

_____

Suggestions from funder: _____

_____

Other suggestions or ideas: _____

_____

_____

Action taken:_____

_____

Follow-up/Comments:_____

_____

_____

Results:_____

_____

THE
IRRESISTIBLE
BUSINESS
PLAN
&
GRANT
WRITING
MADE EASY

LEARNING

www.ingramcontent.com/pod-product-compliance
Lightning Source LLC
Chambersburg PA
CBHW051329170526
45166CB00002B/739